S. Hrg. 113–596

ASSURED ACCESS TO SPACE

JOINT HEARING

BEFORE THE

SUBCOMMITTEE ON STRATEGIC FORCES

OF THE

COMMITTEE ON ARMED SERVICES AND COMMITTEE ON COMMERCE, SCIENCE, AND TRANSPORTATION UNITED STATES SENATE

ONE HUNDRED THIRTEENTH CONGRESS

SECOND SESSION

JULY 16, 2014

Printed for the use of the Committee on Armed Services

Available via the World Wide Web: http://www.fdsys.gov/

U.S. GOVERNMENT PUBLISHING OFFICE

93–719 PDF   WASHINGTON : 2015

For sale by the Superintendent of Documents, U.S. Government Publishing Office
Internet: bookstore.gpo.gov   Phone: toll free (866) 512–1800; DC area (202) 512–1800
Fax: (202) 512–2104   Mail: Stop IDCC, Washington, DC 20402–0001

COMMITTEE ON ARMED SERVICES

CARL LEVIN, Michigan, *Chairman*

JACK REED, Rhode Island	JAMES M. INHOFE, Oklahoma
BILL NELSON, Florida	JOHN McCAIN, Arizona
CLAIRE McCASKILL, Missouri	JEFF SESSIONS, Alabama
MARK UDALL, Colorado	SAXBY CHAMBLISS, Georgia
KAY R. HAGAN, North Carolina	ROGER F. WICKER, Mississippi
JOE MANCHIN III, West Virginia	KELLY AYOTTE, New Hampshire
JEANNE SHAHEEN, New Hampshire	DEB FISCHER, Nebraska
KIRSTEN E. GILLIBRAND, New York	LINDSEY GRAHAM, South Carolina
RICHARD BLUMENTHAL, Connecticut	DAVID VITTER, Louisiana
JOE DONNELLY, Indiana	ROY BLUNT, Missouri
MAZIE K. HIRONO, Hawaii	MIKE LEE, Utah
TIM KAINE, Virginia	TED CRUZ, Texas
ANGUS KING, Maine	

PETER K. LEVINE, *Staff Director*
JOHN A. BONSELL, *Minority Staff Director*

———

SUBCOMMITTEE ON STRATEGIC FORCES

MARK UDALL, Colorado, *Chairman*

JACK REED, Rhode Island	JEFF SESSIONS, Alabama
CLAIRE McCASKILL, Missouri	DEB FISCHER, Nebraska
JOE DONNELLY, Indiana	DAVID VITTER, Louisiana
ANGUS KING, Maine	MIKE LEE, Utah

———

COMMITTEE ON COMMERCE, SCIENCE, AND TRANSPORTATION

JOHN D. ROCKEFELLER IV, West Virginia, *Chairman*

BARBARA BOXER, California	JOHN THUNE, South Dakota, *Ranking*
BILL NELSON, Florida	ROGER F. WICKER, Mississippi
MARIA CANTWELL, Washington	ROY BLUNT, Missouri
MARK PRYOR, Arkansas	MARCO RUBIO, Florida
CLAIRE McCASKILL, Missouri	KELLY AYOTTE, New Hampshire
AMY KLOBUCHAR, Minnesota	DEAN HELLER, Nevada
MARK BEGICH, Alaska	DAN COATS, Indiana
RICHARD BLUMENTHAL, Connecticut	TIM SCOTT, South Carolina
BRIAN SCHATZ, Hawaii	TED CRUZ, Texas
EDWARD MARKEY, Massachusetts	DEB FISCHER, Nebraska
CORY BOOKER, New Jersey	RON JOHNSON, Wisconsin
JOHN E. WALSH, Montana	

ELLEN L. DONESKI, *Staff Director*
JOHN WILLIAMS, *General Counsel*
DAVID SCHWIETERT, *Republican Staff Director*
NICK ROSSI, *Republican Deputy Staff Director*
REBECCA SEIDEL, *Republican General Counsel and Chief Investigator*

CONTENTS

ASSURED ACCESS TO SPACE

WEDNESDAY, JULY 16, 2014

U.S. SENATE,
SUBCOMMITTEE ON STRATEGIC FORCES,
COMMITTEE ON ARMED SERVICES;
AND COMMITTEE ON COMMERCE,
SCIENCE, AND TRANSPORTATION,
Washington, DC.

The committees met, pursuant to notice, at 9:29 a.m. in room SH–216, Hart Senate Office Building, Senator Bill Nelson (chairman of the subcommittee) presiding.

Committee members present: Senators Nelson, Udall, Donnelly, Kaine, King, McCain, Sessions, Wicker, Lee, and Cruz.

OPENING STATEMENT OF SENATOR BILL NELSON

Senator NELSON. Good morning. As Senator Udall and Senators Sessions and Cruz arrive, I will recognize them. I want to get this going because we are facing a couple of votes this morning. We are going to have to play this by ear. We will try to keep the hearing going.

It was 45 years ago today that Apollo 11 launched. Most everybody that is a certain age and older in this room will remember exactly where they were on that day, and 4 days later, of course, Armstrong and Collins became the first men to set foot on the moon.

In the decades since, space technology has become vital to our Nation's security, economy, and standard of living. Therefore, it is appropriate that we are holding this hearing to discuss reliable domestic space access, and that is the bottom line of what we are trying to achieve is the goal of assured access to space by American vehicles for both unmanned and manned payloads.

Obviously, the tensions with Russia as a result of the Ukraine crisis have forced us to rethink part of the relationships that have built up and that is despite decades of cooperation, first with the Soviets. Of course, just remember in the midst of the Cold War, an American spacecraft and a Soviet spacecraft rendezvoused, docked, and the crews lived together for 9 days in space. Those crews are good personal friends, and the personal relationship, as exhibited by Tom Stafford and Alexi Leonov, to this day is something to behold.

But when that Cold War ended, we were rightly concerned that a lot of those weapons were going to get into the wrong hands, that a lot of that technology was going to get into the wrong hands. To keep a lot of those former Soviet, now Russian, engineers working,

(1)

there was this extraordinarily successful program of the Nunn-Lugar effort to go in to gather up those nuclear weapons and simultaneously to support the Russian aerospace industry and to buy this incredible engine, the RD–180. Today, those engines play a significant role in meeting our Nation's launch requirements. We have already launched four missions this year alone using that engine.

Now it is time that we have to consider an alternative. Several of us on the Senate Armed Services Committee (SASC) put $100 million into the National Defense Authorization Act (NDAA) to get that process started in this coming fiscal year. We want to make sure that the taxpayers' money is well spent, and so it is important that we consider the launch needs with the goal in mind that we want assured access to space. This is, obviously, not going to just affect the Department of Defense (DOD), although the national security activities are paramount. It clearly is going to involve commercial space activities as well and the question of preserving an industrial base.

The two committees represented on this dais have asked officials from DOD and the National Aeronautics and Space Administration (NASA), along with many others, to come and discuss this issue of U.S. assured access to space. NASA has no stated need for a new engine and is already building its own space launch system (SLS). However, NASA, obviously, has extensive experience in building launch systems and is getting great experience in public/private partnerships. We are going to hear from all of these people.

Now, I am going to short circuit my remarks because we are racing against the clock. We have a 10:15 a.m. vote and then a 12:20 p.m. vote. I am going to call on the chairman of the Strategic Forces Subcommittee of the SASC and the ranking members to give some brief opening remarks, and then we will get into the panel. Your written comments are entered as a part of the record. I am going to ask you to keep it to about 3 minutes each so that we can then get into questions.

Senator Udall.

STATEMENT OF SENATOR MARK UDALL

Senator UDALL. Thank you, Senator Nelson.

In the spirit of Senator Nelson's comments, let me introduce my statement into the record and then make a couple of comments on procedure. Given the number of witnesses and possible member attendance, I would propose to my colleagues that we use 5-minute rounds of questions.

As Senator Nelson pointed out, according to the floor staff, we have a vote at approximately 10:15 a.m. and another at 12:20 p.m. That being the case, I would like to ask that some of my colleagues remain to continue the hearing during the 10:15 a.m. vote while others vote and come back to switch places with them so that they may also go vote. Then we can repeat that procedure for the 12:20 p.m. vote, if it is needed.

Again, I share Senator Nelson's sentiments. It is a very important hearing. I want to thank all of our witnesses for being here today.

[The prepared statement of Senator Udall follows:]

PREPARED STATEMENT BY SENATOR MARK E. UDALL

Thank you, Senator Nelson.

[I would like to recommend for questions we use early bird rule that we use in the Armed Service Committee which is the order of seniority for those present when the gavel falls and order of arrival thereafter.]

I'm proud to join you this morning as we co-chair this joint hearing between the Subcommittee on Strategic Forces of the Senate Armed Services Committee and the Senate Committee on Commerce, Science and Transportation. Today, our committees will hear testimony regarding the effort to maintain assured access to space for civil and military missions. The fact that both committees have such a strong interest in this subject demonstrates how vitally important assured access to space is for our economy, our national security—as well as for our communications, weather forecasts, networks, and scientific efforts.

In light of that reality, we are here to address a number of issues that affect our ability to deliver payloads into orbit. In the interest of time, I'll mention just two of these issues.

First is the ongoing effort to introduce competition into the launch market. Having additional certified competitors in the marketplace will help to lower the cost of delivering payloads into space and will help to drive innovation. We must also ensure that those providers are able to meet the technical requirements necessary to provide mission assurance. The United States makes significant investments in our space-based assets, and we must be absolutely confident that they reach the proper orbit safely.

Second, we should address the recent developments with Russia and our reliance on the Russian-built liquid rocket engines used on the Atlas Five medium lift vehicle. Atlas is a proven workhorse with a tremendous record of success for civilian and military lift. Since the 1990s, U.S. policy has been to stockpile the Russian engine rather than develop a domestic engine. We are now re-evaluating that policy, and I hope the witnesses today can give their views on how to best meet our national needs.

Finally, I'd like to thank all the witnesses for taking the time today to testify. They are experts in their respective fields, and I am looking forward to hearing their views. In particular, I would like to recognize General Shelton, who will retire next month after 38 years in uniform. General, you've been a tireless advocate for a responsible and effective national security space policy— and you've been a great member of the Colorado Springs community. I wish you nothing but the best in your well-earned retirement.

With that, I'll turn to Senator Sessions for his opening statement.

Senator NELSON. Senator Sessions?

STATEMENT OF SENATOR JEFF SESSIONS

Senator SESSIONS. Thank you, Senator Nelson, for your observations and your opening statement.

We are dealing with an important issue. It was not long ago that Russian Deputy Prime Minister Dmitryi Rogozin stated this, "After analyzing the sanctions against our space industry, I suggest the USA to bring their astronauts to the International Space Station using a trampoline."

We do not have assured access to space, as Senator Nelson has raised, and we have to have that. I wish we were not in this situation. I wish we could have avoided it. We are not and we need to make some changes.

The House of Representatives has proposed legislation and identified $220 million in their authorization in appropriations committees to deal with the problem of developing a new rocket engine, which we can do. I am very confident about that. I believe the price is going to be within our reach. Our committee has recommended $120 million. We need to work on that. We need to see if NASA, Mr. Lightfoot, can contribute in this process.

Mr. Chairman, thank you for having the hearing. It is good for us to be together. There are going to be some complexities, but I believe both houses of Congress have already laid out proposals that could work. We have an excellent panel to help us make the right decision as we go forward. Thank you.

Senator NELSON. Thank you, Senator Sessions.

Senator Cruz.

STATEMENT OF SENATOR TED CRUZ

Senator CRUZ. Thank you very much, Mr. Chairman.

I would like to begin by thanking the members of this panel for your service to this country and your efforts to ensure that the United States maintains a strong and capable space presence. The breadth of experience represented by this panel is impressive, and I appreciate your individual contributions towards America's national security.

I also want to thank members of the SASC and the Commerce Committee for recognizing the need to hold a hearing on this issue and its impact on our country's access to space. It remains a simple reality that we need to work closely with the international community to guarantee that the International Space Station (ISS), its mission, and its crew are positively impacted by the decisions made here in Congress. Our astronauts and their peers are relying on a stable partnership to ensure their success.

The block purchase of 36 Evolved Expendable Launch Vehicle (EELV) cores last year may have made economic sense during the global environment at that time and resulted in a meaningful savings, $4.4 billion, to the American taxpayers.

Although well-intentioned, the unintended consequences of relying on a foreign supplier for critical national security equipment is now strikingly apparent. The United States is scrambling to maintain access to space and has no immediate options if the current supplier in Russia decides to cease export or if geopolitical circumstances dictate that the United States is no longer able to engage in a partnership with its supplier.

When the United States decided to utilize a foreign engine, RD–180, to boost our rockets into space, it was also agreed that production of that engine would ultimately occur in the United States. For whatever reason, whether it was for economic reasons or inattention, this never occurred. We find ourselves in this position as a result of our own inaction.

The United States must now respond decisively and provide the domestic capacity to launch both crew and cargo into space. The cost estimates for the design, construction, testing, and certification of a new multi-core engine are staggering in today's climate of limited financial resources. But we simply cannot rely on the vicissitudes of a foreign supplier in a foreign nation for our national security, and therefore we must do what it will take to reduce our reliance on foreign engines.

I look forward to hearing your suggestions, hearing your expertise as we work together on how best to alleviate this issue and defend the interest of the United States.

Thank you, Mr. Chairman.

Senator NELSON. Thank you, Senator Cruz.

Senators, rather than calling on you now, what I will do is I will forego my questions so we can get directly to you after we have heard from the witnesses.

We have the Honorable Alan F. Estevez, Principal Deputy Under Secretary of Defense for Acquisition, Technology, and Logistics. His testimony is going to focus on the current launch portfolio and the efforts to encourage competition and the options.

Next, U.S. Air Force General William L. Shelton, Commander of Air Force Space Command. He will touch on the requirements for launching national security payloads, as well as the challenges presented with the RD–180.

Then, Mr. Robert M. Lightfoot, Jr., NASA Associate Administrator. He will talk about NASA's launch requirements.

On the second panel, we have Ms. Cristina T. Chaplain, Director of Acquisition and Sourcing Management at the Government Accountability Office (GAO). She will discuss the efforts to encourage competition among the government's launch services.

Next, Retired U.S. Air Force Major General Howard J. Mitchell, Vice President for Program Assessments at The Aerospace Corporation.

Next, Mr. Daniel L. Dumbacher, formerly NASA's Deputy Associate Administrator for Exploration Systems Development, now at Purdue.

Finally, Dr. Yool Kim, Senior Engineer at the RAND Corporation, will draw on assessment of risk related to the RD–180.

I welcome all of you on behalf of the Senate, and we will start with you. I know it is compressed to get 3 minutes, but because of the interruption of votes today, it is of necessity and we want to get to questions. Mr. Estevez?

STATEMENT OF HON. ALAN F. ESTEVEZ, PRINCIPAL DEPUTY UNDER SECRETARY OF DEFENSE FOR ACQUISITION, TECHNOLOGY AND LOGISTICS

Mr. ESTEVEZ. Thank you, Senator Nelson.

Chairmen Nelson and Udall, Ranking Members Sessions and Cruz, distinguished members of the committee, I appreciate the opportunity to testify about assuring space access. I want to thank the committees for your providing support for our space-based capabilities. My written testimony has more detail, as you noted, and I ask that it be admitted to the record.

Defense space capabilities are central to our national security. Our assured access to space provides leaders and our men and women in uniform with unprecedented advantages in decision-making, military operations, and homeland security.

Since 2002, DOD has conducted 72 successful EELV missions after refocusing on the importance of mission assurance following a string of failures in the 1990s.

To address concerns over the escalating costs of our national security space launch program, DOD restructured the EELV program in 2012. The restructured program balances efficient procurement of launch services, maintains the focus on mission assurance, and reintroduces competition into the EELV program. The restructured program also enabled the Air Force to award the contract for multiple launch services over a 5-year period. The contract helped stabilize the U.S. launch industrial base and saves the DOD and taxpayers more than $4.4 billion.

To facilitate competition going forward, the program is working with multiple potential new entrants launch service providers to successfully complete the new entrant certification process. The first new entrants could be certified later this year.

Years ago, we chose to utilize the Atlas V with the Russian RD–180 engine as a cost-effective way to meet space launch needs. However, the United States is not dependent on Russian technology to launch our critical space assets. The Delta IV launch vehicle has a domestically produced propulsion system that is capable of lifting all national security payloads. Once certified, new entrants are also expected to be able to lift a portion of the national security manifest using domestically produced propulsion systems. Today the Atlas V contractor, United Launch Alliance (ULA), maintains a reserve stock of RD–180 engines in the United States and will support launches through late fiscal year 2016. Nevertheless, the long-term U.S. national security interests would be enhanced by shifting from the RD–180 to next generation U.S. engines in the most efficient and affordable manner.

The goal of DOD continues to be making space lift more affordable while reaching the advantages of competition. We have implemented the principles of better buying power, saving $4.4 billion, and have set in motion a sound strategy to foster future competition. In addition, DOD will continue to work with our interagency partners in creating an affordable, low-risk plan to reduce the Nation's reliance on Russian-manufactured propulsion systems.

Thank you for the opportunity to discuss our Nation's space launch capability. I look forward to your questions.

[The prepared statement of Mr. Estevez follows:]

PREPARED STATEMENT BY MR. ALAN ESTEVEZ

Chairmen Udall and Nelson, Ranking Members Sessions and Cruz, and distinguished members of the committees, I appreciate the opportunity to testify to you about assuring space access.

INTRODUCTION

Defense space capabilities are central to our national security. Our assured access to space provides national security decision-makers with unfettered global access and unprecedented advantages in national decision-making, military operations, and homeland security. We cannot achieve this without an efficient and reliable space launch capability. The nation requires robust, responsive, and resilient space transportation capabilities that enable and advance our space operations.

REDUCING THE COST OF SPACE LAUNCH

The Evolved Expendable Launch Vehicle (EELV) program has provided launch services for critical national security payloads since 2002 with an unprecedented record of success. The Air Force and the Office of the Secretary of Defense took steps in 2012 to significantly restructure the EELV program based on a significant concern over the escalating cost of domestic space launch. Our goal was to maintain this critical capability through a more cost effective and efficient execution of the program. The Air Force devised a strategy that balances efficient procurement of launch services, maintains mission assurance, and reintroduces competition into the EELV program. The strategy was structured to allow for competition between the United Launch Alliance (ULA) and certified New Entrants as early as possible. As a direct result of this strategy and our concerted efforts to apply Better Buying Power principles to the program, in December of last year, we successfully negotiated and awarded a contract for launch services over 5 years with ULA for the procurement of 36 EELV cores. A core is generally one launch vehicle, with the exception of the Delta IV Heavy, which requires three cores. This contract award has had two significant impacts: (1) it effectively stabilizes the U.S. launch industrial base; and (2) saves the DOD and taxpayers more than $4.4 billion when compared to the fiscal year 2012 President's budget baseline.

Since restructuring the program, we have stopped the burgeoning cost of maintaining a domestic launch capability, without sacrificing the rigor required to maintain mission success, thus concurrently achieving the program's two most important goals. At the same time, the Department is encouraged by the potential for competition to include capable and certified New Entrant launch providers in the years to come.

COMPETITION

The Under Secretary of Defense for Acquisition, Technology, and Logistics approved the Air Force's strategy to reintroduce competition into the EELV program on November 27, 2012. To facilitate competition, the program is working with multiple potential launch service providers, such as Space Exploration Technologies Corporation (SpaceX) and Orbital Sciences Corporation, to successfully complete the New Entrant Certification process. The Air Force received the first Statement of Intent (SOI) from SpaceX on February 7, 2012, and it was revised in August 2012. Subsequently, the first New Entrant Assessment Certification Plan was developed by SpaceX for the Falcon 9 v1.1 launch system and was documented in a joint Air Force/SpaceX Cooperative Research and Development Agreement signed on June 7, 2013. SOIs have also been received and initially assessed for the Orbital Sciences Corporation Antares launch vehicle and the SpaceX Falcon Heavy variant.

The Air Force competitively procured launch services from SpaceX for the joint National Aeronautics and Space Administration (NASA)/National Oceanic and Atmospheric Administration (NOAA) Deep Space Climate Observatory payload and a Space Test Program mission, STP–2 on November 30, 2012, through the Orbital Suborbital Program OSP–3 (non-EELV) contract. These missions allow the New Entrants to provide launch services for lower risk missions to the government while gaining operational experience and exposing them to the Government's Mission Assurance processes. This experience positions a new Entrant, once certified, to compete more effectively for future EELV-class National Security Space (NSS) missions.

Based on the current New Entrant certification schedule, we expect that the SpaceX Falcon 9 v1.1 could be certified to lift NSS missions as early as late 2014. In the meantime, SpaceX will continue to prove its capabilities through a combination of launch operations for NASA and commercial customers along with the launch services already awarded for the more risk tolerant NASA/NOAA Deep Space Climate Observatory and STP–2 missions. The Air Force and National Reconnaissance Office have also issued leading edge integration contracts to SpaceX for several NSS missions in advance of their actual certification. These contracts are just one more active step the Department is taking to ensure that once a New Entrant, such as SpaceX, is certified as an EELV provider, they will be prepared to compete for NSS launch services. The Air Force is also working with other potential new entrants, such as Orbital Sciences Corporation, that are in various stages of the certification process. In support of the Department's effort to aggressively introduce competition at the earliest opportunity, we have included a request to realign $100 million in the fiscal year 2014 Omnibus Reprogramming for additional competitive launch procurement in fiscal year 2015.

MISSION ASSURANCE

The Department of Defense has conducted 72 successful EELV missions since 2002, after refocusing on the importance of Mission Assurance following a string of failures in the late 1990s. The Department intends to retain this focus on Mission Assurance as we reintroduce competition into the Department's EELV program and evaluate the options for future rocket propulsion. In cooperation with each of the prospective EELV New Entrants, we are implementing a multi-step certification process designed to ensure all new launch service providers meet the existing high U.S. Government levels of design and operational reliability prior to awarding a NSS launch service certification. The Mission Assurance process has evolved over the last 15 years into a flexible and efficient process that is tailored to a particular set of mission requirements based on the risk tolerance of the payload to be launched. We intend to continue to evolve this process as new entrants are on-ramped into the EELV program.

USE OF THE RUSSIAN RD–180 ROCKET ENGINE

The United States is not dependent or reliant on Russian technology to launch our critical space assets. The Delta IV launch vehicle has a domestically produced propulsion system that is capable of lifting all national security payloads. Additionally, once certified, New Entrants are expected to be able to lift a large portion of the NSS manifest. The ultimate goal is the entire manifest being competed using domestically produced propulsion systems.

Approximately 18 years ago, we chose to utilize the Atlas V with the Russian RD–180 engine as a cost effective way to meet the National Space Transportation Policy Assured Access to Space policy.

As a result of the recent Russian aggressive action in the Ukraine, we have begun to reevaluate our utilization of the Russian manufactured RD–180 rocket engine. The RD–180 rocket engine is used to power the Atlas V first stage and provides access to space for critical national security space payloads. There were sound policy and cost saving reasons for the original decision to allow the incorporation of this engine into a U.S. launch vehicle. One of the considerations explicitly addressed at the time of that decision—and periodically since that time—was the risk associated with utilizing a non-U.S.-manufactured article for a critical national security capability. Recent events have renewed our existing concerns with this practice.

The Department believes the Nation needs to eliminate our utilization of Russian propulsion systems in the most efficient and affordable manner possible. This requires evaluation of a range of alternatives. For this reason, and because the possibility of an engine supply interruption continues to exist, the Department initiated a review of the options available in order to mitigate a supply interruption, should it occur. The study included evaluating both immediate- and longer-term responses to a potential interruption of supply; including re-manifesting of missions to the Delta IV launch vehicle, evaluating the options for developing a new domestically produced engine, as well as the possible utilization of EELV New Entrants to supplement existing government space lift capability. The Department continues to evaluate the range of mitigation measures for the longer term. The study clearly identified that any deviation from the current program of record will require a significant near-term investment. As an initial step, the Department has requested $40 million be reprogrammed to initiate engine risk reduction activities. Today, the incumbent contractor, ULA, maintains a Reserve stock of engines in the United States. Currently there are 15 in stock, with an expected delivery of 5 more before the end of the year, which will support launches through late fiscal year 2016. In addition, as noted above, we have maintained an alternative domestic capability with the Delta IV variant of the EELV to launch national security payloads. That capability will be increased and diversified as new U.S. providers are certified to launch national security payloads. Nevertheless, the long-term U.S. national security interests, and those of significant elements of our space industrial base, would be enhanced by shifting to next generation U.S. developed engines.

CONCLUSION

The goal of the Department has been, and continues to be, to stabilize the EELV program to make spacelift more affordable while leveraging the advantages of competition. We have accomplished this goal by implementing the principles of Better Buying Power, saving over $4.4 billion for the taxpayer since the fiscal year 2012 President's budget, and setting in motion a sound strategy to foster future competition. We will continue to stress the importance of mission assurance that has already resulted in 72 straight successful EELV launches.

The continued use of Russian manufactured propulsion systems has been and continues to be a difficult question. The Department will continue to work with its partners in creating an affordable and technically low-risk plan to reduce the Nation's use of Russian manufactured rocket propulsion systems. Once we have formalized our preferred approach, we will be happy to return and share it with you and your staff.

Thank you again for this opportunity to discuss the Nation's space launch capability. I look forward to answering your questions.

Senator NELSON. Thank you.
General Shelton?

STATEMENT OF GEN. WILLIAM L. SHELTON, USAF, COMMANDER, AIR FORCE SPACE COMMAND

General SHELTON. Chairman Nelson, Chairman Udall, Senator Cruz, Senator Sessions, and distinguished members of both committees, it is a pleasure to represent Air Force Space Command here today.

It is also my privilege to appear with distinguished colleagues on the panel.

The Air Force's space capabilities are foundational to the joint warfighter and the Nation's capabilities who collectively rely on these systems across the range of civil and military operations. It is critical then that we ensure space services continue to be available at the times and places of our choosing, even in an increasingly challenged space domain. Ensuring these space services continue to be available starts with assured access to space.

Our ultimate objective is to safely and reliably place national security payloads on a schedule determined by the needs of the national security space enterprise. We are proud to have established an unprecedented launch success record with our EELV program by placing an uncompromising premium on mission assurance.

Additionally, we have worked hard to reduce costs in our acquisition strategy with our current provider, ULA, and by progressively introducing competition into the launch business. But we must continue to insist on thorough, system engineering-based mission assurance processes. The loss of even one national security payload, both in terms of financial loss and operational impact, would make our mission insurance costs look like very cheap insurance. To make sure we sustain our incredible track record of success, we will continue to treat each and every launch as if it is our first.

Commensurate with the EELV's success, the commercial space launch industry has made substantial progress over the last year, including successful launches by Orbital Sciences and SpaceX. As a result, we are managing change in the EELV program from a single-provider environment to a multi-provider environment through a disciplined certification process. Through this process, we will continue to carefully and conservatively manage the introduction of full and open competition to ensure planned and future missions are delivered safely, successfully, and on schedule.

I thank you for your support, and I look forward to working with Congress to provide resilient, capable, and affordable space capabilities for the joint force and for the Nation. Thank you.

[The prepared statement of General Shelton follows:]

PREPARED STATEMENT BY GEN. WILLIAM L. SHELTON, USAF

INTRODUCTION

The Air Force's space capabilities—and the airmen who operate them—are foundational to our Nation's ability to deter aggression and effect global impact across the entire range of civil and military operations, from humanitarian and disaster relief through major combat. Our military satellites provide mission-critical global access, persistence and awareness for our national security and have become vital to the global community and world economy as well. Space assets have been a key element of warfighting for over 30 years, providing a unique vantage to observe activity around the globe, relay terrestrial communications, and provide precision position information.

The challenge before us, then, is to ensure space services continue to be available, at the times and places of our choosing, even in an increasingly challenging space domain. The first step in this process is to assure our ability to provide safe, reliable, and available access to space for national security payloads. We have established an unprecedented launch success record by placing an uncompromising premium on mission assurance. Not that many years ago, we took our collective eyes off mission assurance and paid dearly for it. The loss of even one national security payload-both in terms of financial loss and operational impact-would make our mission assurance costs look like very cheap insurance. Therefore, we will continue to place emphasis on tough mission assurance principles to do all that is humanly possible to guard against launch failure.

THE EVOLVED EXPENDABLE LAUNCH VEHICLE PROGRAM

By 2010, the Evolved Expendable Launch Vehicle (EELV) program predicted significant cost growth. Mainly, this was due to the sharply rising price of launch vehicle propulsion systems due to excess industrial capacity and resulting infrastructure costs in the wake of the retirement of the Space Shuttle program. Another cosi driver was the established practice of procuring launches individually, driving business uncertainty to the U.S. domestic launch industrial base, and particularly, the rocket propulsion industry. In response, working with the Secretary of Defense and Congress, the Air Force initiated a 36-core block buy with United Launch Alliance (ULA)—the single certified industry provider at the time—but also documented a plan to expand the program's provider base through the carefully managed introduction of competition. This approach reserves missions for future competition, while focusing on maintaining a full spectrum national security launch manifest.

The Air Force has intensified attention on the business aspects of the EELV program to control costs while maintaining a 100 percent mission success rate since 1999. This year's budget reduces the program by $1.2 billion. Combined with prior-year Air Force reductions and savings for the National Reconnaissance Office, we have reduced the total program by $4.4 billion from the baseline in the fiscal year 2012 budget.

COMPETITIVE NEW ENTRANT ENVIRONMENT

The commercial space launch industry has made substantial progress over the last year, including successful launches by Orbital Sciences and SpaceX. As a result, we are managing change in the EELV program from a single-provider environment to a multi-provider environment through a certification process. When industry entrants seek to compete for Department of Defense (DOD) launches, they understand and agree to a set of statutory and regulatory requirements that every DOD program contractor is required to fulfill to enter into competition. The certification process ensures all prospective industry entrants meet the program's baseline technical requirements, which include accommodation for existing payload designs, ability to launch to specific orbits, and desired launch dates (for projected missions). All requirements that are part of the certification process are validated through the DOD requirements process. This ensures Department oversight of processes and program costs, and helps to minimize mission risk.

Our launch acquisition strategy aims to take advantage of the competition made possible by capable new entrants, once certified according to the approved new entrant certification process. Planning space missions involves a significant investment in both financial and personnel resources over multiple years. The certification strategy, jointly developed by the Air Force, National Aeronautics and Space Administration (NASA), and the National Reconnaissance Office (NRO), ensures that once certified, new entrants to the market have earned Department confidence of meeting current and future mission needs. The phased introduction of competition through deliberate certification is the approach chosen to help lower launch costs while maintaining a laserlike focus on mission assurance. We are also striving to encourage a stable and reliable industrial base to ensure continued assured space access.

In Phase 1 of the current EELV program, the Air Force, alongside our NRO and Navy partners, agreed to acquire 36 cores from ULA over a period of 5 years (between fiscal years 2013–2017) [note: one core means one launch vehicle, with the exception of the Delta IV Heavy, which is three cores]. The contract provides a stable business base to our current provider, as well as the ability to conduct economic order quantities with their subcontractors. It is important to note that the scope of the 36-core buy was set by our assessment of which cores and missions we would have to buy from ULA. In executing the block buy, we reserved as many missions as possible for competition between certified providers.

While increases in satellite service-life and budget realities have reduced the previously planned number of missions viable for competition, Air Force efforts to foster a robust competitive environment have not flagged. It remains our intent to make as many launches as possible available for competition during Phase 1A and beyond.

Phase 2 introduces a wider variety of competition options, and reflects an environment in which every DOD launch is competed between certified launch providers. Air Force Space Command's Space and Missile Systems Center continues to refine this acquisition strategy while looking forward to Phase 3 in the 2023–2030 timeframe. Although the only certified launch provider today is ULA, the Air Force has committed considerable budget and manpower resources to facilitate new entrant certification. Through this process, we will continue to carefully and conservatively manage the introduction of competition to ensure that planned and future missions are delivered safely, successfully, and on schedule.

FOREIGN ENGINE RELIANCE AND MITIGATION

In addition to efforts to certify other vehicle families, the Air Force recently completed an RD–180 Availability Risk Mitigation Study at the request of the Secretary of Defense. This study found that an RD–180 production loss or interruption would have significant impact on our ability to reliably launch the current manifest of national security payloads on a schedule of our choosing. While the study does evaluate a number of near-term (fiscal year 2014–2017) options to mitigate RD–180 supply disruption—including options to use the RD–180 inventory stockpile, adjust the currently planned manifest to use of alternate launch vehicles, increase alternative launch vehicle production rates, and/or even re-sequence or delay some missions— no option is risk-free, and certainly not cost-free. A prolonged interruption would result in increased risk for our national security space posture due to unavoidable delays. Options are limited in part to the current state of new entrants in the certification process; in other words, the lack of certified additional vehicles at this time. There is also risk and cost associated with the engineering and lead-time necessary to transfer existing Atlas V missions—those using the RD–180—to the more expensive Delta IV launch vehicle as well. The current inventory of RD–180 engines is expected to last up to 2 years in the event of supply disruption, while sustaining the manifest.

While DOD and the Air Force conlinue to evaluate the range of potential mitigation measures, the Air Force has already begun work to ensure our near-term launch requirements continue with minimal disruption should RD–180 engine availability become an issue. We are developing both near- and far-term strategies to explore alternatives, and place at a premium the continued exploration of both competition and public-private partnerships to drive innovation, stimulate the industrial base, and reduce costs.

While the RD–180 has served us well, current uncertainty highlights the need to consider other options for assured access to space. If deemed a national priority, a sustained focus on rocket propulsion technology would allow the United States to operate within a broader trade space, helping mitigate disruptive events affecting external supply lines. A domestically produced new engine program would revitalize the liquid rocket propulsion industrial base, end reliance on a foreign supplier, and aid the competitive outlook for the entire domestic launch industry. Such an undertaking would be a multi-year effort, however, and would require significant congressional support to maintain adequate funding in future years.

CONCLUSION

Air Force payloads provide foundational space capabilities to the Joint Warfighter and the Nation, who collectively rely on these systems across a range of civil and military operations. We are committed to sustaining the highest levels of mission assurance, and our ultimate objective is to safely and reliably launch national security payloads on a schedule determined by the needs of the national security space enterprise.

We have an incredible track record of success, but to ensure we maintain this record, we will continue to treat each and every launch as if it is our first. We thank the committees for their support and look forward to our continued partnership to provide resilient, capable, and affordable space capabilities for the Joint Force and the Nation.

Senator NELSON. Thank you.
Mr. Lightfoot?

STATEMENT OF ROBERT M. LIGHTFOOT, JR., ASSOCIATE ADMINISTRATOR, NATIONAL AERONAUTICS AND SPACE ADMINISTRATION

Mr. LIGHTFOOT. Thank you, Chairman Nelson, Chairman Udall, and other distinguished committee members. I appreciate the opportunity to testify before you on NASA's plans for ensuring access to space. My written testimony has been submitted for the record.

NASA has embarked on an ambitious path to send humans to Mars. This path includes conducting research aboard the ISS, developing the SLS, Orion crew vehicle, and testing our new capabilities in the proving ground of cis-lunar space. We continue to do this with the cooperation from my international partner community.

As a critical element in this long-term exploration strategy, expanding commercial access to low earth orbit (LEO) and extensive utilization of the ISS are among NASA's highest priorities. We will rely on and partner with U.S. industry and international partners for access to ISS while seeking to encourage innovation and to maintain a competitive environment for these services.

NASA continues to make strong progress on the SLS, an exploration class heavy-lift launch vehicle designed for missions far beyond LEO. The SLS will begin with a lift capability of 70 metric tons, evolving to 105 metric tons, and eventually up to 130 metric tons. Near-term human exploration missions will benefit most from an enhanced upper stage. Increased booster thrust performance is not required until NASA undertakes more significant human missions such as landing on the surface of Mars. Our current needs do not require or have a need for a new LOX/hydrocarbon booster engine risk reduction or development effort at this time.

Through fiscal year 2020, NASA has plans to launch over 18 science missions of various size classes. We anticipate that our commercial launch service providers will add additional launch vehicles to our NASA launch services contract at some point in the near future.

NASA currently plans to launch payloads on six commercially provided Atlas V rockets which rely on the Russian-supplied RD–180 engines. Should the supply of these engines be disrupted, an interagency discussion would be required in order to allocate the available remaining RD–180s among national security and NASA considerations. Other launch vehicles would need to be considered using the appropriate procurement processes that we have in place.

NASA continues to work with our partners in DOD as it assesses approaches that could increase production rates and potentially reduce costs for launch systems that do not rely on the RD–180. We are committed to working with our partners to provider safe, reliable, and cost-effective access to space.

Mr. Chairman, thank you again for the opportunity to appear today, and I would be happy to respond to any questions you may have.

[The prepared statement of Mr. Lightfoot follows:]

Mr. Chairman, thank you for this opportunity to testify before you on National Aeronautics and Space Administration's (NASA) plans for access to space. NASA's requirements for access to space are driven by the agency's broader goal to expand the frontiers of science and human exploration of space. As part of the overall strategy to meet this goal, and consistent with the national consensus described by the NASA Authorization Act of 2010, the Agency is pursuing a stepping-stone approach to the human exploration of space leading to human missions to Mars in the 2030s. As key steps along this path to Mars, NASA will continue research aboard the International Space Station (ISS), develop the Space Launch System (SLS) and Orion crew vehicle, and test our new capabilities in the proving ground of cis-lunar space.

As a critical element in this long-term exploration strategy, and also supported by existing policy and law, expanding commercial access to low-earth orbit (LEO) and commercial, exploration, and scientific utilization of the ISS remain among NASA's highest priorities. With the administration's commitment to the extension of ISS operations through 2024, NASA looks forward to expanded research opportunities and commercial transportation of both cargo and crew to and from ISS. Currently, two American companies are launching cargo to the ISS from U.S. soil. This summer, NASA will complete a commercial crew competition and we will select one or more commercial companies to develop the capability to launch American astronauts from American soil by the end of 2017. Competition is a key to controlling costs over the long-term as well as to improving the level of safety and NASA will seek to maintain competition to the degree feasible.

NASA is developing the next generation of scientific missions in pursuit of our Nation's space and Earth science goals. Through fiscal year 2020, NASA has plans to launch over 18 science missions of various size classes on a variety of launch vehicles.

SPACE ACCESS BEYOND LOW-EARTH ORBIT

The SLS is an exploration-class, heavy-lift launch vehicle that will transport the Orion crew vehicle, as well as cargo and other systems, and is uniquely designed for missions beyond LEO. SLS will begin with a lift capability of 70 metric tons, evolving to 105 metric tons and eventually up to 130 metric tons, based on future mission requirements. The evolution of the SLS lift capability fulfills specific, important roles within the Nation's and the emerging global exploration architecture, enabling human exploration missions to Mars and similarly challenging expeditions.

Our analysis indicates that near-term human exploration missions will benefit most from increased "in-space" performance from an enhanced upper stage. Increased booster thrust performance will further supplement that capability, but it is not required until NASA undertakes human missions to even more challenging deep-space destinations such as the surface of Mars. NASA is committed to evolving the SLS vehicle system capability with an enhanced upper stage and/or advanced booster (solid or liquid) in the future, but our current needs do not require funding for a new liquid-oxygen/hydrocarbon booster engine risk reduction or development effort at this time. We plan to use our remaining risk reduction funding in fiscal year 2015 and beyond to conduct enhanced liquid hydrogen fueled upper stage work. The results of our investments in risk reduction will be available to, and can be leveraged by, other interested Government organizations.

Although NASA's expected mission needs do not require a new booster engine at this time, we will monitor the development actions of our sister agencies to understand how their work could support future NASA requirements. We continue to work with DOD to assess the overall U.S. launch posture and are reviewing how NASA's unique facilities and expertise and experience might best contribute to future development efforts.

ACCESS TO THE INTERNATIONAL SPACE STATION

Under NASA's Commercial Resupply Services (CRS) contracts, Space Exploration Technologies (SpaceX) has been selected to provide 12 cargo flights to the ISS, and Orbital Sciences Corporation (Orbital) has been selected to provide 8 flights. Counting demonstration flights and CRS resupply flights, SpaceX has now completed three cargo missions to the ISS, successfully delivering cargo and returning scientific samples to Earth, with the fourth mission expected to launch in the third quarter of this year. Orbital Sciences Corporation has completed their demonstration mission to the ISS and their first contract mission under CRS to deliver crew supplies, research and other cargo onboard the Cygnus spacecraft. Orbital launched its second ISS resupply mission just last week. NASA continues to work with its commercial partners to develop a U.S. commercial capability for human spaceflight, and remains committed to its goal of launching American astronauts from U.S. soil by the end of 2017. 2014 will be a pivotal year for NASA's Commercial Crew Program (CCP), as the Agency is preparing to announce one or more awards in August/September for Commercial Crew Transportation Capability contracts that will include operational crewed flights to the ISS. In addition to helping NASA meet mission requirements, a number of lessons learned and other experiences are being gained through these public-private ventures.

SPACE ACCESS FOR OTHER NASA AND NATIONAL MISSIONS

NASA's Launch Services Program (LSP) within the Human Exploration and Operations Mission Directorate supports the Agency's diverse scientific mission portfolio by working diligently to match spacecraft with the right industry launch vehicles for optimal mission success and Government efficiency.

NASA Launch Services (NLS) contracts are the primary contractual mechanisms LSP uses to acquire commercial launch services to place NASA-owned and NASA-sponsored robotic missions, payloads, and/or spacecraft into orbit. The current series of NASA Launch Service contracts, known as NLS II contracts, are Firm Fixed Price, Indefinite Delivery/Indefinite Quantity, Federal Acquisition Regulation, Part 12, type contracts. NLS II has an ordering period through June 2020, with a period of performance through December 2022. In order to compete for task orders to launch NASA science payloads, commercial launch service companies must first be qualified to receive a contract under NLS II. Task orders are competed across the NLS II contract holders for the launch of a specific NASA mission.

NASA has in its portfolio a variety of domestic launch vehicles which will carry out various missions launching new and exciting payloads to study the Earth and the solar system, all the while maintaining our state-of-the-art Space Communications and Navigation network. The portfolio of rockets available to the Agency through the NASA Launch Services contract managed by LSP includes the UnitedLaunchAlliance-provided Atlas V and Delta II; the SpaceX provided Falcon 9 v1.1; the Orbital-provided Antares 120, Antares 130, Minotaur-C (formerly known as the Taurus XL) and Pegasus XL; and the Lockheed Martin Athena IIc and Athena Ic. In addition, LSP anticipates that our commercial launch service providers will add additional launch vehicles (such as the Delta IV and the Delta IV Heavy) and new launch vehicles (such as the Falcon Heavy) to our NASA Launch Services contracts at some point in the near future so those commercial launch services can compete to launch NASA's missions.

FUTURE BOOSTER ENGINE REQUIREMENTS

Recent geopolitical events have highlighted the dependence of some U.S. launch vehicles upon Russian-supplied RD–180 liquid oxygen/hydrocarbon engines. However, NASA anticipates that available alternative launch vehicles could effectively substitute for NASA launches now planned utilizing the RD–180 engine, and is working with our Department of Defense partners to assess all manifest options and cost impacts should that become necessary.

As has been described above, NASA does not have a current requirement for a liquid-oxygen/hydrocarbon engine in support of the SLS now in development at this time. With respect to CRS for the ISS, CCP, and LSP supporting the launch of our Agency and other civil-sector satellites, NASA expects commercial providers to propose and provide launch solutions that are consistent with national policy, and for our commercial cargo and satellite launch service providers to meet their contractual commitments.

NASA currently plans to launch payloads on six commercially provided Atlas V rockets which rely on Russian supplied RD–180 engines. Should the supply of these engines be disrupted, an interagency discussion would be required in order to allocate the available remaining RD–180 engines among national security and NASA missions. Other launch vehicles would need to be considered using appropriate procurement procedures, which would add time to the launch process. This process would entail significant fiscal impacts caused by the program delays required in order to make the necessary mission-to-launch vehicle assignment changes. However, any Government-funded program to develop an engine to replace the RD–180 would also require a substantial investment of funds over a significant period of time. NASA will advise DOD efforts to initiate rocket engine risk reduction activities that could lead to a possible development effort. NASA will also continue to work with the DOD on ongoing strategic assessments of the overall U.S. space propulsion and transportation industrial base and believes such assessments should be completed before any decision is made to fund a new engine. This includes considering approaches that could concentrate on improving current system production rates and reduce per unit costs while maintaining high reliability and increasing competition, as well as considering the significant investments that the Nation has made (and the international leadership we have carefully developed and maintained) over the past several decades in key propulsion technologies, such as liquid hydrogen and solid propulsion.

In summary, NASA relies on an array of vehicles to access space. The Agency is developing a uniquely capable heavy-lift launch vehicle, has contracts with commercial partners for cargo services in support of the ISS, is working with commercial partners to develop a commercially-provided crew capability for LEO, and has contracts with commercial providers for the launch of scientific and other civil payloads. NASA recognizes the threat posed by a potential disruption in the supply of the RD–180 engine and we are moving forward to work with other Government agencies on options to address this threat. We continue to work with the DOD as it assesses approaches that could increase production rates and potentially reduce costs for launch systems that do not rely on the RD–180 engine. Mr. Chairman, thank you for the opportunity to appear before you today. I would be happy to respond to any questions you may have.

Senator NELSON. Thank you.
Ms. Chaplain?

STATEMENT OF CRISTINA T. CHAPLAIN, DIRECTOR, ACQUISITION AND SOURCING MANAGEMENT, GOVERNMENT ACCOUNTABILITY OFFICE

Ms. CHAPLAIN. Chairman Udall, Chairman Nelson, Ranking Member Cruz, Ranking Member Sessions, and distinguished members of the committees, thank you for inviting me to participate in today's hearing.

I would just like to make three points about our relevant work.

First, as our testimony indicates, in the past we have highlighted deficiencies in the management and oversight of the EELV, as well as gaps in knowledge needed for the block buy that is now in place. Both DOD and Congress have taken significant steps to rectify the problems we identified. For instance, DOD undertook rigorous efforts to obtain greater insight into program costs in advance of its contract negotiations with ULA. It took steps to reinstitute oversight reporting for the program, and it completed a new cost estimate. Over time, DOD has also come to recognize the value of competition for the EELV program, noting that with no threat of competition DOD was in a poor negotiating position.

Second, with respect to the current competition, we have reported on the benefits and the challenges associated with how DOD could run the competition, but we did not recommend a specific approach as that decision should be made by DOD based on its requirements and resources. Important factors include the need to maintain a high degree of reliability, as the satellites being launched are expensive and vital to national security, the need for flexibility in launch scheduling, the importance of retaining cost and pricing data, the need to keep costs down, and considerations about the government's future demand for launch services.

Third, my testimony identifies best practices that should be adopted in future rocket engine or launch vehicle development efforts. The one I would like to stress here is the need for decisions to be made with a government-wide perspective and a long-term perspective. Our work has shown that defense and civilian government agencies together expect to require nearly $44 billion for the next 5 years for launch activities. At the same time, our past work has found that launch acquisitions and activities have not always been well-coordinated, though DOD and NASA have made progress on that front since then. Concerns have also been raised in various studies about the lack of strategic planning and investment for future technologies. Further, industry is at a crossroad with new vendors emerging and certain strategic capabilities and less demand by the government. The bottom line is that any new launch vehicle effort is likely to have impacts that reach beyond DOD and the EELV program and should be carefully considered in a government-wide and long-term context.

This concludes my statement. I look forward to answering your questions.

[The prepared statement of Ms. Chaplain follows:]

PREPARED STATEMENT BY MS. CRISTINA CHAPLAIN

Chairmen Rockefeller and Udall, Ranking Members Thune and Sessions, and members of the committee and subcommittee:

Thank you for inviting me to testify on the current and future state of the U.S. launch enterprise. The Evolved Expendable Launch Vehicle (EELV) program is the primary provider of launch vehicles for U.S. military and intelligence satellites. Today I will discuss: (1) highlights of Government Accountability Office's (GAO) past work on EELV; and (2) how acquisition best practices would benefit future engine development efforts. In general, our past work has highlighted a need for stronger management and oversight for EELV as well as more knowledge about pricing, costs and the industrial base for the block buy. DOD and Congress have implemented many positive actions to address our recommendations. For future efforts, adopting best practices early could help stem cost and schedule growth and other problems.

My testimony is based on the body of work we have performed on the EELV program and acquisition best practices in recent years and related reports issued from September 2008 to March 2014. In this body of work we interviewed DOD and industry officials, conducted contract reviews, assessed knowledge of the industrial base, and analyzed program acquisition strategies, among other things. Our prior reports each include a detailed description of our scope and methodology. All work on which this testimony is based was performed in accordance with generally accepted government auditing standards. Those standards require that we plan and perform the audit to obtain sufficient, appropriate evidence to provide a reasonable basis for our findings and conclusions based on our audit objectives. We believe that the evidence obtained provides a reasonable basis for our findings and conclusions based on our audit objectives.

The Department of Defense (DOD) expects to spend about $9.5 billion over the next 5 years acquiring launch hardware and services through the program, during which time it will also be working to certify new launch providers. This investment represents a significant amount of what the entire U.S. Government expects to spend on launch activities—including new development, acquisition of launch hardware and services, and operations and maintenance of launch ranges—for the same period. The United Launch Alliance (ULA) is currently the sole provider of launch services through the EELV program. However, DOD, the National Aeronautics and Space Administration (NASA), and the National Reconnaissance Office (NRO) are working to certify new launch providers who can compete with ULA for launch contracts.

HIGHLIGHTS OF GAO'S WORK ON EELV

Because of the importance of the national security space launch enterprise, we have been asked to look at many aspects of the EELV program over the last 10 years. Our work has examined management and oversight for EELV, as well as the "block buy" acquisition approach. The block buy approach, finalized in December 2013, commits the department to an acquisition that spans 5 years, in contrast with the prior practice of acquiring launch vehicles one or two at a time, with the aim of stabilizing the launch industrial base and enabling the government to achieve savings. Additionally, we have assessed the status of the launch vehicle certification process for new entrants. DOD and Congress have taken numerous actions to address our prior recommendations which have resulted in financial and oversight benefits. Highlights of our work over the years follow.

2008

We reported that when DOD moved the EELV program from the research and development phase to the sustainment phase in the previous year, DOD eliminated various reporting requirements that would have provided useful oversight to program officials and Congress.[1] For example, the EELV program was no longer required to produce data that could have shed light on the effects the joint venture between Lockheed Martin and Boeing companies (later known as ULA) was having on the program, programmatic cost increases and causes, and other technical vulnerabilities that existed within the program. Furthermore, because the program was now in the sustainment phase, a new independent life-cycle cost estimate was not required for the program; as a result, DOD would not be able to rely on its estimate for making long-term investment planning decisions. According to DOD officials, the life-cycle cost estimate for the program at the time was not realistic. Our recommendations to strengthen oversight reporting gained attention in 2011 following concerns about rising program cost estimates and at that time, Congress required the Secretary of Defense to redesignate the EELV program as a major defense acquisition program, thereby removing it from the sustainment phase and reinstating previous reporting requirements. DOD also developed a new program cost estimate, which allows for greater oversight of the program for both Congress and DOD.

2011

We reported that the block buy acquisition approach may be based on incomplete information and although DOD was still gathering data as it finalized the new acquisition strategy, some critical knowledge gaps remained.[2] Specifically, DOD analysis on the health of the U.S. launch industrial base was minimal, and officials continued to rely on contractor data and analyses in lieu of conducting independent analyses. Additionally, some subcontractor data needed to negotiate fair and reasonable prices were lacking, according to Defense Contract Audit Agency reports, and some data requirements were waived in 2007 in exchange for lower prices. DOD also had little insight into the sufficiency or excess of mission assurance activities, which comprise the many steps taken by the government and contractors to ensure launch success. Though the level and cost of mission and quality assurance employed today is sometimes criticized as excessive, it has also resulted in more than 80 consecutive successful launches. We also reported that the expected block buy may commit the government to buy more booster cores than it needs, and could result in a surplus of hardware requiring storage and potentially rework if stored for extended periods.[3] Further, while DOD was gaining insight into the rise in some engine prices, expected at that time to increase dramatically, it was unclear how the knowledge DOD was gaining would inform the expected acquisition approach or subsequent negotiations.

We reported that broader issues existed as well, regarding the U.S. Government's acquisition of, and future planning for, launch services—issues which we recommended be addressed, given that they could reduce launch costs and assure future launch requirements are met. For example, we recommended that Federal agencies—like the Air Force, NRO, and NASA—more closely coordinate their acquisitions of launch services. Planning was also needed for technology development focused on the next generation of launch technologies, particularly with respect to engines, for which the United States remains partially reliant on foreign suppliers. Congress responded to our work by legislating that DOD explain how it would address the deficiencies we found.

2012

We reported that DOD had numerous efforts underway to address the knowledge gaps and data deficiencies identified in our 2011 report.[4] Of the seven recommendations we made to the Secretary of Defense, two had been completely addressed, four were partially addressed and one had no action taken. That recommendation was aimed at bolstering planning for the next generation of launch technologies. Since GAO's 2011 report, DOD had completed or obtained independent cost estimates for two EELV engines and completed a study of the liquid rocket engine industrial

---

[1] GAO, Space Acquisitions: Uncerlainties in the Evolved Expendable Launch Vehicle Program Pose Management and Oversight Challenges, GA0–08–1039 (Washington, DC: Sept. 26, 2008).

[2] GAO, Evolved Expendable Launch Vehicle: DOD Needs to Ensure New Acquisition Strategy Is Based on Sufficient Information, GA0–11–641 (Washington, DC: Sept. 15, 2011).

[3] The booster core is the main body of a launch vehicle.

[4] GAO, Evolved Expendable Launch Vehicle: DOD Is Addressing Knowledge Gaps in Its New Acquisition Strategy, GA0–12–822 (Washington, DC: July 26, 2012).

base. Officials from DOD, NASA, and the NRO initiated several assessments to obtain needed information, and worked closely to finalize new launch provider certification criteria for national security space launches. Conversely, we reported that more action was needed to ensure that launch mission assurance activities were not excessive, to identify opportunities to leverage the government's buying power through increased efficiencies in launch acquisitions, and to strategically address longer-term technology investments.

2013

We reported on the status of DOD's efforts to certify new entrants for EELV acquisitions.[5] While potential new entrants stated that they were generally satisfied with the Air Force's efforts to implement the process, they identified several challenges to certification, as well as perceived advantages afforded to the incumbent launch provider, ULA. For example, new entrants stated that they faced difficulty in securing enough launch opportunities to become certified. During our review, the Under Secretary of Defense for Acquisition, Technology, and Logistics directed the Air Force to make available up to 14 launches for competition to new entrants, provided they demonstrate the required number of successful launches and provide the associated data in time to compete. Additionally, new entrants considered some Air Force requirements to be overly restrictive; for example, new entrants must be able to launch a minimum of 20,000 pounds to low earth orbit from specific Air Force launch sites (versus facilities the new entrants currently use.) The Air Force stated that 20,000 pounds represents the low end of current EELV lift requirements, and that alternate launch sites are not equipped to support DOD's national security space launches. Further, new entrants noted that the incumbent provider receives ongoing infrastructure and development funding from the government, an advantage not afforded to the new entrants, and that historical criteria for competition in the EELV program were more lenient. The Air Force acknowledged that criteria for competition are different, and reflective of the differences in the current acquisition environment.

2014

We reported and testified that DOD's new contract with ULA (sometimes referred to as the "block buy") represented a significant effort on the part of DOD to negotiate better launch prices through its improved knowledge of contractor costs, and that DOD officials expected the new contract to realize significant savings, primarily through stable unit pricing for all launch vehicles.[6] At the time of our review, DOD was leading the broader competition for up to 14 launches, expected to begin in fiscal year 2015. In advance of the upcoming competition, DOD was considering several approaches to how it would require competitive proposals to be structured. Our report did not recommend an approach. However, we identified the pros and cons of two different ends of the spectrum of choices, one being a commercial-like approach and the other being similar to the current approach (a combination of cost-plus and fixed price contracts). If DOD required offers be structured similar to the way DOD currently contracts with ULA, there could be benefits to DOD and ULA as both are familiar with this approach, but potential burdens to new entrants, which would have to change current business practices. Alternatively, if DOD implemented a commercial approach to the proposals, new entrants would potentially benefit from being able to maintain their current efficient business practices, but DOD could lose insight into contractor cost or pricing, as this type of data is not typically required by the Federal Acquisition Regulation under a commercial item acquisition. DOD could also require a combination of elements from each of these approaches, or develop new contract requirements for this competition.

BEST PRACTICES WOULD BENEFIT FUTURE ENGINE DEVELOPMENT EFFORTS

ULA's Atlas 5 launch vehicle uses the RD–180 engine produced by the Russian company NPO Energomash. DOD and Congress are currently weighing the need to reduce U.S. reliance on rocket engines produced in Russia and the costs and benefits to produce a similar engine domestically. The RD–180 engine has performed extremely well for some of the Nation's most sensitive national security satellites, such as those used for missile warning and protected communications. Moreover, the

---

[5] GAO, Launch Services New Entrant Certification Guide, GA0–13–317R (Washington, DC: Feb. 7, 2013).
[6] GAO, The Air Force's Evolved Expendable Launch Vehicle Competitive Procurement, GA0–14–377R (Washington, DC: Mar, 4, 2014) and GAO, Evolved Expendable Launch Vehicle: Introducing Competition into National Security Space Launch Acquisitions, GA0–14–259T (Washington, DC: Mar. 5, 2014).

manufacture process of the RD–180 is one that cannot be easily replicated. In addition, the most effective way to design a launch capability is to design all components in coordination to optimize capabilities needed to meet mission requirements. In other words, replacing the RD–180 could require the development of a new launch vehicle and potentially new launch infrastructure.

Space launch vehicle development efforts are high risk from technical, programmatic, and oversight perspectives. The technical risk is inherent. For a variety of reasons, including the environment in which they must operate, a vehicle's technologies and design are complex and there is little to no room for error in the fabrication and integration process. Managing the development process is complex for reasons that go well beyond technology and design. For instance, at the strategic level, because launch vehicle programs can span many years and be very costly, programs often face difficulties securing and sustaining funding commitments and support. At the program level, if the lines of communication between engineers, managers, and senior leaders are not clear, risks that pose significant threats could go unrecognized and unmitigated. If there are pressures to deliver a capability within a short period of time, programs may be incentivized to overlap development and production activities or delete tests, which could result in late discovery of significant technical problems that require more money and ultimately much more time to address. For these reasons, it is imperative that any future development effort adopt disciplined practices and lessons learned from past programs. I would like to highlight a few practices that would especially benefit a launch vehicle development effort.

First, decisions on what type of new program to pursue should be made with a government-wide and long-term perspective. Our prior work has shown that defense and civilian government agencies together expect to require significant funding, nearly $44 billion in then-year dollars (that factor in anticipated future inflation), for launch-related activities from fiscal years 2014 through 2018.[7] At the same time, our past work has found that launch acquisitions and activities have not been well coordinated, though DOD and NASA have since made improvements.[8] Concerns have also been raised in various studies about the lack of strategic planning and investment for future launch technologies. Further, the industry is at a crossroads. For example, the government has a decreased requirement for solid rocket motors, yet for strategic reasons some amount of capability needs to be sustained and exercised. The emergence of Space Exploration Technologies, Corp. (SpaceX) and other vendors that can potentially compete for launch acquisitions is another trend that benefits from coordination and planning that takes a government-wide perspective. The bottom line is that any new launch vehicle effort is likely to have effects that reach beyond DOD and the EELV program and should be carefully considered in a long-term, government-wide context.

Second, requirements and resources (for example, time, money, and people) need to be matched at program start. This is the first of three key knowledge points we have identified as best practices. In the past, we have found that recent launch programs, such as NASA's Constellation program and Commercial Crew Program, have not had sufficient funding to match demanding requirements.[9] Funding gaps can cause programs to delay or delete important activities and thereby increase risks and can limit the extent to which competition can be sustained. Realistic cost estimates and assessments of technical risk are particularly important at program start. Space programs have historically been optimistic in estimating costs (although recently DOD and NASA have been making strides to produce more realistic estimates). The commitment to more realistic, higher confidence cost estimates would be a great benefit to any new launch vehicle development program and enable Congress to ensure its commitment is based on sound knowledge. We have also found that imposing overly ambitious deadlines can cause an array of problems. For instance, they may force programs to overlap design activities with testing and production.[10] The many setbacks experienced by the Missile Defense Agency's ground-based midcourse defense system, for example, are rooted in schedule pressures that

[7] GAO, Defense and Civilian Agencies Request Significant Funding for Launch-Related Activities, GA0–13–802R (Washington, DC: Sept. 9, 2013).

[8] GAO, 2012 Annual Report: Opportunities to Reduce Duplication, Overlap and Fragmentation, Achieve Savings, and Enhance Revenue, GA0–12–342SP (Washington, DC: Feb. 28, 2012).

[9] GAO, NASA: Constellation Program Cost and Schedule Will Remain Uncertain Until a Sound Business Case Is Established, GA0–09–844 (Washington, DC: Aug., 26, 2009) and GAO, NASA: Actions Needed to Improve Transparency and Assess Long-Term Affordability of Human Exploration Programs, GA0–14–385 (Washington, DC: May 8, 2014).

[10] GAO, Missile Defense: Mixed Progress in Achieving Acquisition Goals and Improving Accountability, GA0–14–351 (Washington, DC: Apr. 1, 2014).

drove concurrent development.[11] Even if the need for a new engine is determined to be compelling, the government is better off allowing adequate time for disciplined engineering processes to be followed.

Third, the program itself should adopt knowledge-based practices during execution. The program should also use quantifiable data and demonstrable knowledge to make go/no-go decisions, covering critical facets of the program such as cost, schedule, technology readiness, design readiness, production readiness, and relationships with suppliers. Our work on the second and third knowledge points during execution (design stability and production process maturity) has tied the use of such metrics to improved outcomes. In addition, the program should place a high priority on quality, for example, holding suppliers accountable to deliver high-quality parts for their products through such activities as regular supplier audits and performance evaluations of quality and delivery, among other things. Prior to EELV, DOD experienced a string of launch failures in the 1990s due in large part to quality problems.

This concludes my statement. I am happy to answer questions related to our work on EELV and acquisition best practices.

Senator NELSON. Thank you.
General Mitchell?

STATEMENT OF MAJ. GEN. HOWARD J. MITCHELL, USAF (RET.), VICE PRESIDENT, PROGRAM ASSESSMENTS, THE AEROSPACE CORPORATION

Mr. MITCHELL. Chairman Nelson, Chairman Udall, thank you for this opportunity to speak and I also thank the rest of the members that are attending the hearing.

I was asked to do a study on the RD–180 mitigation study. I recently chaired that under a terms of reference that was signed by the Assistant Secretary of the Air Force for Acquisition. I have provided the committee a version of that briefing for the record, as well as my opening comments.

I will just hit the four major areas that the study identified.

First, a disruption of the RD–180 engine could have significant impact on the United States' ability to launch DOD, Intelligence Community, NASA, National Oceanic and Atmospheric Administration, and commercial satellites scheduled to launch on Atlas V through 2020. Neither the Delta IV nor new entrants can help mitigate that impact until 2017 and beyond.

Second, there are several upcoming events that bear monitoring as they can provide indications of the Russians' intent and the United States' intent.

Third, the current Air Force strategy for competition can be adversely affected should the Atlas not be available for competition.

Fourth, in the 2022–2023 timeframe with appropriate near-term funding for technology maturation, the Nation could have new launch capabilities based on liquid oxygen/hydrogen engine technology that do not rely on foreign sources.

I look forward to answering any questions you might have.

[The prepared statement of Mr. Mitchell follows:]

---

[11] GAO–14–351. In 2004 we found that the Missile Defense Agency (MDA) committed to a highly concurrent development, production, and fielding ground-based midcourse (GMD) interceptors. Because MDA moved forward with interceptor production before completing its flight testing program, test failures have exacerbated disruptions to the program. For example, because the program has delivered approximately three-fourths of the interceptors for fielding, the program faced difficult and costly decisions on how it will implement corrections from prior test failures. Also, the program has had to add tests that were previously not planned and delay tests that are necessary to understand the system's capabilities and limitations. As a result of these development challenges, the GMD program will likely continue to experience delays, disruptions, and cost growth.

PREPARED STATEMENT BY MAJOR GENERAL HOWARD "MITCH" J. MITCHELL, USAF (RET.)

Co-chairs, thank you and good morning. Members of the committees, good morning, and thanks for the opportunity to discuss the RD–180 Mitigation Study that I recently chaired under a Terms of Reference signed by the Assistant Secretary of the Air Force (Acquisition). I have provided the committees with a version of the briefing that has been previously released to the committees and the contractors that supported the study.

The Terms of References requested that the effects of the potential non-availability of Russian built RD–180 be examined and that the worst case scenario, as well as others, be presented along with near-term and far-term recommendations for mitigation. The Study panel was also asked to look at implications for other than the Department of Defense (DOD) users, impacts to the industrial base, costs, et cetera.

The major findings of the study fall in four categories; (1) a disruption of RD–180 engines would have a significant impact on the United States' ability to launch, DOD, Intelligence Community, National Aeronautics and Space Administration (NASA), National Oceanic and Atmospheric Administration (NOAA), and commercial satellites scheduled to launch on Atlas V through 2020; and that neither Delta IV or New Entrants can mitigate the impact until 2017 and beyond; (2) there are several upcoming events that bear monitoring as they can provide indications of the Russian, and United States, intents; (3) that the current Air Force strategy for competition can be adversely affected should the Atlas not be available for competition; and (4) that in the 2022–2023 timeframe with appropriate near-term funding for technology maturation, the Nation could have new launch capabilities based on Liquid Oxygen/Hydrocarbon engine technology.

The committees asked that I address the following topics:

(1) Discuss the government-wide implication of the various scenarios we investigated.

- The worst case scenario we examined was that the recent Atlas V launch, May 22, 2014, would be the last RD–180 launch due to Russian actions, congressional actions, court actions or a catastrophic failure that the Russians would not assist in resolving. While it does not appear that any of the above is occurring, it is the worst case scenario.

  i. The Government-wide implications of this scenario are 2–3 year delays in satellite launches and several billion dollars in cost.
  ii. A second implication is that the launch order of the satellites would need to be addressed in an interagency process and would affect the DOD, Intelligence Community, NASA, NOAA, and commercial missions.
  iii. Third, the planned Evolved Expendable Launch Vehicle (EELV) competition would be adversely affected because the Atlas V would not be available, and the Delta IV production could not be ramped up fast enough to provide addition launch system to compete (all Delta IVs would be needed to recover from the launch delays).

- The second scenario we examined was that the RD–180 engines in stock would be allowed to fly out in the current order, but no additional RD–180s could be used.

  i. This scenario results in fewer launch delays for a shorter period, but is not the optimal use of RD–180 engines due to the fact that some Atlas V missions would be driven to fly on a Delta IV Heavy, which is a much more expensive alternative.

- The third scenario we examined was that the RD–180 engines in stock would be allowed to fly out in an optimum launch order but no additional RD–180s could be used.

  i. This scenario results in fewer launch delays for a shorter period, and is the optimal use of RD–180.
  ii. Additionally, the launch order of the satellites would need to be addressed in an interagency process and would affect the DOD, Intelligence Community, NASA, NOAA, and commercial missions.

(2) Options for pursuing a domestic propulsion system.

- The Study team recommended that the Government invest in critical technologies needed to mature Liquid Oxygen/Hydrocarbon engines and make that technology available to industry.

  i. A decision on Engineering and Manufacturing Development would not need to be made until fiscal year 2017, but funding would have to be laid in during the fiscal year 2016 POM development.

ii. Other options exist depending on the viability (i.e., does the business case close) of the Industrial Base—the Study did not have time to delve into an Acquisition Strategy, but did acknowledge that public-private partnership should be pursued.

(3) Overview of potential commercial partners for launch system development.

- We were briefed by all the contractors in the engine and launch system business and feel that a healthy environment would exist for competition. It was not clear how much Government funding and/or oversight would be necessary.

- We did provide a worst case estimate of how much the development of a totally new launch system would cost, but if the program was tailored after the original EELV program the costs could be substantially less. However, we did not have time to investigate this further than the worst case.

(4) Discuss any other relevant issues.

- The only other issue I would like to briefly discuss is that the development of a Liquid Hydrogen/Hydrocarbon engine is a national decision to reverse a decision we made when the Government agreed to allow the RD–180 engine to be used on the Atlas V.

i. The Government essentially decided to outsource large (1 million pounds of thrust at altitude) Liquid Oxygen/Kerosene engine procurement and significantly scale back U.S. technology investment.

ii. Having an entire suite of propulsion options (Solid Rocket Motors, Liquid Oxygen/Liquid Hydrogen, Liquid Hydrogen/Hydrocarbon) for future launch vehicle development available allows the designers to optimize the launch system design for the mission requirements. The missions that the EELV is designed for are very different than the mission requirements that the Space Launch System is being designed to meet.

Senator NELSON. Thank you, General.
Mr. Dumbacher?

STATEMENT OF DANIEL L. DUMBACHER, PROFESSOR OF PRACTICE, DEPARTMENT OF AERONAUTICS AND AERO-SPACE ENGINEERING, PURDUE UNIVERSITY

Mr. DUMBACHER. Chairman Nelson, Chairman Udall, and members of today's respective committees, thank you for the opportunity to discuss the current state of the U.S. launch enterprise.

The United States' ability to achieve and go beyond LEO is essential for our Nation's defense, commercial, and space exploration enterprises.

Leaving the surface of the Earth and attaining orbital velocity at 17,500 miles per hour is a complex systems challenge. Factors key to achieving this task are mission requirements, technical performance, development risk and cost, operations cost, schedule, industrial base, and yes, even political concerns, which all must be addressed with multiple stakeholders.

In the early phase of a rocket launch, thrust is more important to initially overcome the Earth's gravity than propulsion efficiency. However, as the vehicle progresses to higher altitudes and climbs out of the Earth's gravity well, propulsion efficiency becomes more important, even as thrust remains an important technical parameter.

When NASA was preparing to go to the moon in the 1960s, it determined that large amounts of thrust were needed for the first 2½ minutes of flight to put the Apollo spacecraft and lunar lander on the surface of the moon. To meet the mission need, NASA recognized that much development and testing effort of liquid oxygen/kerosene systems was required and therefore restarted the Air Force's E–1 development from the 1950s as the F–1 program.

During the development of the Space Shuttle, NASA determined that it had a lower payload delivery requirement and constrained budgets. The development cost estimates for the shuttle's solid booster were lower than competing booster liquid systems. Many of the same challenges were again considered by NASA during the planning and development process for the SLS. NASA assessed many launch configurations, weighing the pros and cons of each. Again, technical performance, challenges associated with limited budgets, the need to launch the first flight as early as possible, and impacts to the propulsion industrial base weighed heavily on NASA's decisionmaking.

Ultimately for the SLS, NASA determined that using the solid boosters based on shuttle and constellation experience minimized the upfront development costs, reduced the development risks, and most likely would result in a more timely first flight of the SLS. NASA also chose to utilize over 40 years of investment in large liquid oxygen/liquid hydrogen engines to minimize development cost and risk.

Following the Apollo program, the U.S. Government dramatically limited its hydrocarbon investments and focused on utilizing solid propulsion systems and liquid oxygen/liquid hydrogen systems. The United States leads the world in these propulsion systems. However, we need to reduce the costs of these systems. In my opinion, the United States should build upon its long investment in solid and liquid oxygen/liquid hydrogen propulsion systems and allow the marketplace to provide viable choices for use by NASA and DOD. Competition will incentivize industry to develop efficient management models, use the new technologies that will reduce costs, and continue to search for and develop technologies necessary to reduce development and operations costs.

Thank you for allowing me to appear before you today. More details are included in the submitted written testimony. I will be happy to answer your questions.

[The prepared statement of Mr. Dumbacher follows:]

PREPARED STATEMENT BY MR. DANIEL L. DUMBACHER

Chairman Nelson, Chairman Udall, and members of today's respective committees, thank you for the opportunity to discuss the current state of the U.S. launch enterprise on this, the 45th Anniversary of Apollo 11's launch to the Moon.

The United States' ability to achieve, and go beyond, low-Earth orbit is essential for our Nation's defense, commercial, and space exploration enterprises. The U.S. rocket propulsion industry, including solid and liquid propulsion, as well as launch vehicle design, development and operations, is critical to applications such as strategic and tactical systems and serves as our highway to space.

Throughout my 30-year career in the launch vehicle and propulsion business, ranging from my experience with the National Aeronautics and Space Administration (NASA) prior to the first Space Shuttle flight, to my efforts in helping to lead NASA's current development efforts of the Space Launch System and the Orion crew capsule, I have learned several significant lessons. One key lesson is that leaving the surface of the Earth and attaining orbital velocity at 17,500 miles per hour is a complex system challenge that continues to test the best of American ingenuity. Some of the many factors key to achieving this task are: technical performance, development risk, development cost, operations cost, schedule, industrial base, and yes, even political concerns—all must be assessed with multiple stakeholders. All of these factors must be considered alongside the extremely complex technical interactions and challenges.

From the technical perspective, all systems must work together to achieve orbital velocity. For example, in designing a launch vehicle, the design team must integrate propulsion systems with propellant tanks, structures, launch loads environments, thermal environments, computers and software, and the logistics of getting the many subsystems from suppliers to assembly facilities and launch facilities. All of these factors affect the technical design of a launch vehicle, in addition to the budget and schedule requirements. I'd like to focus my testimony today on launch systems, propulsion systems, and why certain design decisions were made for past and current vehicles.

In assessing design options, there are phases of the launch ascent to orbit where different propulsion systems better serve the needs of a particular launch vehicle, in a particular phase of flight, for a specific mission. For example, in the early phase of a rocket launch, thrust is more important to initially overcome the Earth's gravity than propulsion efficiency. However, as the vehicle progresses to higher altitudes, and climbs out of the Earth's gravity well, propulsion efficiency becomes more important, even as thrust remains an important technical parameter. This is the fundamental reason that Apollo's Saturn V used liquid oxygen and kerosene. It is also the reason the Space Shuttle used solid propulsion for the initial 2 minutes of flight in parallel with the liquid oxygen/liquid hydrogen Space Shuttle Main Engines (RS–25). The point being that for initial phases of a launch, solid and liquid oxygen/ kerosene systems perform the necessary functions, and liquid oxygen/liquid hydrogen serve the needs better for upper stages and in space stages, appropriate to the mission.

So the question is, why are different launch systems needed? For example, why did the Saturn V use liquid oxygen/kerosene, and the Space Shuttle use solid propulsion? Why has NASA chosen the current Space Launch System configuration? Mission requirements drive the process. When NASA was preparing to go to the Moon in the 1960s, it determined that large amounts of thrust (~7.5 million lbs. at liftoff) were needed for the first 2.5 minutes of flight, to put the Apollo spacecraft and lunar lander on the surface of the Moon. To meet the mission need, NASA recognized that much development and testing effort of liquid oxygen/kerosene systems was required, and therefore restarted the Air Force's E–1 development from the 1950s as the F–1 program.

In comparison, during development of the Space Shuttle, NASA determined that it had a lower payload delivery requirement and less need for large liquid oxygen/ kerosene systems. This decision was certainly influenced, as are most policy decisions, by constrained budgets. This meant building the safest and most capable system possible, based on specific mission requirements, within budget limits. When NASA was developing the Space Shuttle, solid propulsion was being used by the Titan system and other Defense Department strategic systems. Therefore, NASA determined that these solid systems could be scaled up to meet the Shuttle requirements, thus allowing the Agency to take advantage of an existing solid propulsion industrial base to help reduce development and lifecycle cost. The development cost estimates for the Shuttle's solid booster were approximately $1 billion, (in early 1970 dollars) which was lower than competing liquid propulsion systems. While NASA also recognized that operations costs for the solids would be larger over the life of the Space Shuttle Program, the trade-off was that near-term development costs were more manageable, and near-term budgets were likely more achievable, given that upfront development costs would be less.

Recently, many of the same challenges weighed during the Apollo and Shuttle development eras, were again considered by NASA during the planning and development process for the new Space Launch System. When beginning to design what would become the Space Launch System, NASA looked at many launch configurations, weighing the pros and cons of each. Again, technical performance, challenges associated with limited budgets, the need to launch the first flight as early as possible, and impacts to the propulsion industrial base weighed heavily in NASA's decisionmaking.

Ultimately, for the Space Launch System, NASA determined that using the solid boosters, based on Space Shuttle experience and Constellation/Ares development of the five-segment booster, minimized the upfront development costs, reduced the development risks, and most likely would result in a more timely first flight of the Space Launch System. NASA had also demonstrated, over 110 Space Shuttle flights, that solid propulsion issues resulting in the Challenger disaster had been addressed. In addition, NASA chose to utilize over 40 years of investment in large liquid oxygen/liquid hydrogen engines, and 16 available RS–25s from the Space Shuttle Program, to minimize development cost and risk. As NASA proceeds through the Space Launch System evolution from the 70 metric ton (mt) to the 130 mt system, operations costs are an important factor. NASA's plan is to conduct a full and open competition for the booster system development, between solid and liquid systems, for the 130 mt vehicle. This competition will be requirements-driven, with NASA making proposed development and operations costs a key decision criteria in terms of which companies will be ultimately selected to do the work.

Following the Apollo Program, the U.S. Government focused on utilizing solid propulsion systems and liquid oxygen/liquid hydrogen systems, limiting its hydrocarbon investments. The U.S. aerospace base reacted by focusing its investments in these areas. Major investment decisions made by owners of key propulsion systems affect other users. For example, the RS–68 used today on the Delta IV shares a significant amount of its supply chain with the Shuttle's RS–25, and therefore, increased use of the RS–68 will have the favorable effect of reducing per unit costs on the RS–25. Another example would be the interdependency of the NASA solid propulsion use and supply chain with the U.S. Navy's Strategic Missile D–5 fleet and most Defense tactical systems.

It is clear that cost growth associated with access to space and propulsion is a major threat to the competitive U.S. launch posture. Therefore, it is essential that the U.S. rocket propulsion industry directly and aggressively address launch system costs, working to drive down the cost to develop and operate launch vehicles and propulsion systems.

The question in front of us now, in my opinion, is how do we best utilize this Nation's precious financial resources to address the U.S. launch and propulsion needs? I would submit that focusing our attention on reducing operations costs of propulsion systems will have the most significant, long-term, beneficial outcome for the Nation, thus improving the United States' ability to get to space and assure longterm U.S. launch competitiveness. We also need to address concerns of skill atrophy as our current aerospace workforce ages or changes careers. In my opinion, these challenges are best addressed with technology investments directed toward addressing the operations costs, and do not require full development programs. Investments in new manufacturing techniques such as selective laser melting, 3–D printing, and building and testing the hardware developed with these technologies are critical to furthering the technology and retaining the needed skill base. Use of more efficient government/industry management models, designs meant to reduce operations costs, along with the new manufacturing technologies are also needed.

In conclusion, our national competitive spirit and history of ingenuity has proven, and will continue to prove, to be the best tool to reduce costs while maintaining, and even improving, services and products. The United States should build upon its long investment in solid and liquid oxygen/liquid hydrogen propulsion systems, and allow the marketplace to provide viable choices for use by NASA and the Department of Defense. Competition will incentivize industry to develop efficient management models, use the new technologies that will reduce costs, and continue to search for and develop technologies necessary to reduce development and operations costs.

Thank you for allowing me to appear before you today to share my testimony, and I would be happy to take your questions.

Senator NELSON. Thank you.
Dr. Kim?

STATEMENT OF DR. YOOL KIM, SENIOR ENGINEER, THE RAND CORPORATION

Dr. KIM. Mr. Chairmen, ranking members, and distinguished committee and subcommittee members, thank you for the opportunity to testify before you today on this important issue.

Today, I will focus on the conclusions of a RAND study mandated by Congress on the national security implications of continuing to use foreign components for launch vehicles under the EELV program. I will discuss risks of using foreign components under the EELV program and the potential effects on the U.S. space launch capability and national security space missions if an interruption in the supply of those components should occur.

The Atlas V and the Delta IV launch vehicles in the EELV program have several major foreign components or subsystems and many more lower tier components from countries all over the world. The risk of potential supply interruption of most foreign components in the EELV program is low and manageable.

The foreign component of most concern is the Russian RD–180 engine, the primary booster of the Atlas V launch vehicle. The RD–180 engine supplier poses a moderate risk of a supply interruption primarily related to the political concerns with Russia, although the supplier has strong financial incentives to continue deliveries to ULA. The RD–180 engine is the most critical component in terms of costs, schedule, and the technical difficulty associated with developing an alternative engine source. An interruption in the RD–180 engine supply would cause a significant disruption in EELV launch operations because a large number of Atlas V launches are scheduled in the next few years, and a significant effort would have to be made to mitigate the disruption.

Should a long-term interruption in the RD–180 engine supply occur, risks to the U.S. space launch capability could be mitigated by using the stockpile of RD–180 engines that ULA maintains and by moving some satellites carried on the Atlas V to Delta IV until a new entrant launch vehicle from a different launch service provider or a re-engined Atlas V becomes available. However, the mitigation efforts have significant costs implications and relying on a single launch vehicle would pose a higher risk to U.S. access to space. More details on the mitigation approach and remaining risks are described in my written testimony.

Although some national security space satellites are likely to be delayed during disruption, the risk will be low for most national security space missions if national security space satellites are given priority in use of the RD–180 engine stockpile, particularly for the launch of the critical satellites on Atlas V. However, many variables will influence the mitigation approach which should be based on a consideration of the tradeoffs regarding the cost and schedule and the mission risks of different options.

Again, thank you for inviting me here today to testify on this very important national issue. I look forward to your questions.

[The prepared statement of Dr. Kim follows:]

PREPARED STATEMENT BY DR. YOOL KIM [1]

RISKS AND MITIGATION OPTIONS REGARDING USE OF FOREIGN COMPONENTS IN U.S. LAUNCH VEHICLES [2]

Mr. Chairmen, ranking members, and distinguished committee and subcommittee members, thank you for the opportunity to testify before you today on this important issue.

My testimony today will focus on the key findings from the RAND research [3] on the implications of using foreign components in the Evolved Expendable Launch Vehicle (EELV) program. This study, mandated by Congress, was commissioned out

[1] The opinions and conclusions expressed in this testimony are the author's alone and should not be interpreted as representing those of RAND or any of the sponsors of its research. This product is part of the RAND Corporation testimony series. RAND testimonies record testimony presented by RAND associates to Federal, State, or local legislative committees; government-appointed commissions and panels; and private review and oversight bodies. The RAND Corporation is a nonprofit research organization providing objective analysis and effective solutions that address the challenges facing the public and private sectors around the world. RAND's publications do not necessarily reflect the opinions of its research clients and sponsors.

[2] This testimony is available for free download at http://www.rand.org/pubs/testimonies/CT413.html.

[3] Section 916 of the National Defense Authorization Act for Fiscal Year 2013 directed the Under Secretary of Defense for Acquisition, Technology, and Logistics (USD [AT&L]) to conduct an independent study to assess the potential risk of using foreign components in the EELV program. The Space and Intelligence Office in the Office of the USD(AT&L) asked the RAND National Defense Research Institute to help in such a study, and this report constitutes RAND's response to that request.

of concern that the U.S. launch vehicle fleet depends on foreign components—most notably, the Russian RD–180 engine, the primary booster engine for the Atlas V rocket. I will identify the foreign components in the EELV program, describe the supply risk of these components, and assess the potential effects of supply interruptions on U.S. space launch capability and national security space missions.

FOREIGN COMPONENTS IN THE EELV LAUNCH VEHICLES

Both the Atlas V and Delta IV launch vehicles in the EELV program have complex supply chains with hundreds of participants, both U.S.-based and foreign. An interruption in their supply for the EELV could prevent the launch of critical national security space assets.

There are five major foreign components in the EELV. The RD–180 engine, the primary booster in all Atlas V launch vehicles, is supplied by NPO Energomash, a Russian company largely owned by the Russian Government. The payload fairing, the interstage adapter, and the payload adapter system in certain Atlas V variants are supplied by RUAG, a Government-owned Swiss company. The fuel tank on certain Delta IV variants is supplied by Mitsubishi Heavy Industries, a publicly held Japanese company. Some Delta IV launch vehicles also use the RUAG payload adapter system.

Lockheed Martin chose the RD–180 engine for its Atlas V launch vehicle because of its proven track record of success (based on the flight history of its predecessor engine), performance, and lower cost. The U.S. Government was actively pursuing space cooperation with Russia in the 1990s and encouraged private-sector cooperation with Russia and other former Soviet Union states because of proliferation concerns.

The RD–180 engine is the most critical foreign component in terms of cost, schedule, and the technical difficulty of developing an alternative engine source. Other foreign components pose less risk: the cost and timelines associated with acquiring alternative sources for them would be less stressing, though not insignificant.

RISK OF SUPPLY INTERRUPTION

A supply interruption could occur for a number of reasons, including financial problems, production delays, and political disputes. We found the risk of financial problems or production delays is not that different for foreign and U.S. suppliers. Although NPO Energomash shows evidence of financial problems, it also has strong financial incentives to continue deliveries to United Launch Alliance (ULA). Moreover, in the event of financial distress or bankruptcy, it might be able to continue to operate under protection from its creditors, or its assets could be sold to other firms to avoid supply interruptions. NPO Energomash might also receive funding from the Russian Government, the primary owner of the company. Production risks from product failures, industrial accidents, labor strikes, and natural disasters do not occur very frequently, and they do not seem to be higher for foreign suppliers than for U.S. suppliers.

Political factors, however, are a different matter. Foreign policy disputes with Russia in particular pose an uncertain threat. The risk of political conflicts with the other foreign suppliers is low because the United States has some form of defense cooperation (including defense space cooperation) with the countries in which these foreign suppliers' headquarters or production facilities are located. This is not the case with Russia. The only other potential area of concern involves Swiss restrictions on defense exports, but this risk is relatively low because these components are used in space launch vehicles, not in weapon systems.

In addition to the major foreign suppliers mentioned above, many lower-tier foreign suppliers provide complex manufactured components, software, electronics, and raw materials. However, these suppliers do not appear to pose a risk because most of them are located in countries closely allied with the United States, and most of these components have alternative sources. The few components that are sole-source are in France and Germany, close allies of the United States.

MITIGATION MEASURES FOR AN RD–180 ENGINE SUPPLY INTERRUPTION

Despite longstanding concerns about reliance on the Russian engine, ULA has not experienced any major disruptions in the acquisition of the RD–180 itself. Since the first launch of Atlas V 12 years ago, the few minor problems with RD–180 engines have never caused either a delay in the launch of an Atlas V or a launch failure. Nevertheless, given the concerns within the Department of Defense and Congress, various mitigation measures have been developed in case the supply of RD–180 engines is interrupted.

Maintaining a stockpile of at least 2 years' supply of RD–180 engines has been a risk-mitigation strategy since the beginning of the program. The stockpile provides a hedge against short-term supply interruptions. In the event of a supply interruption that lasts longer than 2 years, the Air Force would need to move some Atlas V satellites onto Delta IVs and increase production of Delta IV launch vehicles while an alternative engine for the Atlas V is being developed. Two launch vehicle families are required for the EELV program according to the United States' assured-access-to-space policy.

A number of alternative liquid oxygen/hydrocarbon engine designs exist within the U.S. rocket engine industrial base, but they are in their infancy. The development cost of an alternative engine can be expected to be on the order of $1 billion and could take about 6 years. These engines could also require modifications to the Atlas V launch vehicle because the engine loads might differ from those of the RD–180 engine. Thus, the cost, schedule, and risk implications of developing a new engine must include the effects on the launch vehicle.

All these options have cost implications. Ramping up production of Delta IVs could entail additional manufacturing costs. It could take a few years to ramp up depending on how quickly the manufacturer could accelerate the manufacturing and supply-chain capability to increase production. It might also be necessary to invest in launch infrastructure at Cape Canaveral Air Force Station to support increased Delta IV launches that would minimize launch delays of national security space missions.

Domestic production of the actual RD–180 engines in the United States is another possible mitigation measure, but this option may not be desirable because it is only marginally better than developing a completely new engine in terms of cost and technical challenges.

In addition to these measures, other domestic launch vehicles are emerging that may be able to meet some of EELV launch needs. Although not technically a mitigation for a RD–180 supply interruption, a new space launch entrant increases the options available for assured access to space. SpaceX's Falcon 9 launch vehicle has made the most progress in the new entrant certification process and, once certified, it may be able to launch some of the satellites currently carried on Atlas V, although the first launch may not occur until 2 years after certification.[4] SpaceX's Falcon Heavy would be required to launch all the satellites carried by Atlas V, but this launch vehicle is not as far along in the new entrant certification process as Falcon 9.

Even with the mitigation measures in place, however, there are other risks that the U.S. space launch capability might temporarily face during a RD–180 engine supply interruption. First, the engine design expertise lies within NPO Energomash, and access to that expertise may not be possible during a supply interruption driven by political disputes. If this is the case, the United States may not have the technical expertise needed to resolve RD–180 engine anomalies in a timely manner during the transition period. Second, any unexpected delays in the availability of an alternative launch vehicle, either a re-engined Atlas V or a new-entrant launch vehicle, could undermine U.S. assured-access-to-space capability. If the Delta IV launch vehicle family were to encounter a problem during the transition period, the United States could temporarily lose the capability to launch national security space satellites until the problem was resolved. Third, while the Atlas V launch vehicle production is being ramped down during the transition to an alternative engine, the supplier base for the Atlas V could be affected. Some suppliers could disappear, depending on their level of reliance on Atlas V production. Weakening of the industrial base could lead to potential delays in delivering re-engined Atlas V launch vehicles.

EFFECTS OF FOREIGN SUPPLY INTERRUPTION ON U.S. SPACE LAUNCH CAPABILITY

Because the United States is launching a larger number of satellites for the next few years, its vulnerability to a supply interruption, particularly of RD–180 engines, is likely to be highest now and in the immediate future. A supply interruption of the other foreign components is likely to pose only a minor disruption because these components are only used in some—not all—of the Atlas V and Delta IV launch vehicles and the mitigation options (i.e., the number of components in stockpile and flexibility to move the satellites from the affected launch vehicle to another launch vehicle) can minimize launch delays. But an RD–180 engine supply interruption could cause a serious disruption in EELV launches because of difficulties in estab-

---

[4] After certification, we assumed it will take an additional 2 years before the first routine NSS launch on Falcon 9, a typical lead time required to prepare a spacecraft to fly on a launch vehicle on which it has never flown.

lishing an alternative engine source and the large number of scheduled Atlas V launches.

If the flow of RD–180 engines were interrupted in the near-term, the stockpile would be sufficient to last about 2 years without further mitigation efforts. An interruption that lasts longer than 2 years—or is permanent—will require moving many satellites currently carried on the Atlas V to Delta IVs. The current Air Force contingency plan would call for Atlas V operations to gradually ramp down and for Delta IV operations to ramp up to support the satellites originally intended to launch on Atlas Vs until a new entrant launch vehicle or a re-engined Atlas V becomes available.

Based on our assumption that national security space launches would take priority over civil and commercial launches, we conclude that the RD–180 engine stockpile appears to be sufficient to protect the launch schedule of a set of Atlas V satellites that are too difficult or too costly to move to Delta IVs. Nevertheless, some national security space launches are likely to be delayed while the Delta IV launch vehicle production ramps up because of the limited number of Delta IV launch vehicles and the limited launch throughput capacity at Cape Canaveral Air Force Station. Decisions about which launches should be delayed would be based on the priority of the national security space mission that the satellite supports and the operational status of the satellite constellation, with inputs from senior U.S. space leadership. We believe the risk these delays would cause is low for most national security space missions. However, we note that many variables will influence the final decision on the mitigation approach and which launches would be delayed. Other assessments of the impact of an RD–180 supply interruption on U.S. space launch capability may differ from ours if they are not based on the same assumptions.

In summary, there are both risks and benefits of using foreign components in the EELV program. The risk of potential supply interruption of most foreign components is low and manageable. The foreign component of most concern is the Russian RD–180 engine, but the impact of an interruption in its supply could be mitigated. Many variables will influence the mitigation approach, which should be based on a consideration of the trade-offs regarding the costs and schedules, and thus mission risks, of different options.

Again, thank you for inviting me here today to testify on this very important national issue. I look forward to your questions.

Senator NELSON. Thank you.

Congratulations, all of you have set a Senate record. [Laughter.]

All seven of you. It leaves time for our Senators to ask questions. I will defer my questions and do cleanup at the end. Other than the chairman and the ranking member, we will call the Senators in order in which they came. Senator Udall?

Senator UDALL. Thank you, Mr. Chairman.

Our mission here as a Congress and a country is to assure access to space for both civil and military missions. Both committees are here because this is so vital. Space access is vital to our economy, our national security, as well as communications, our weather forecast networks, and our scientific efforts. In that context, I want to just touch on two of, I think, key issues that are attached to this mission.

First, is the ongoing effort to introduce competition into the launch market. Having additional certified competitors in the marketplace will help lower the cost of delivering payloads into space and, of course, drive innovation. We must also ensure that those providers—and many of you have spoken to this—are able to meet the technical requirements necessary to provide mission assurance. We make significant investments as a country in our space-based assets and we have to be absolutely confident that they reach the proper orbit safely.

Second, we have to address the recent developments with Russia and our reliance on the Russian-built liquid rocket engine used on the Atlas V medium-lift vehicle. Atlas, as you all know, is a proven workhorse with a tremendous record of success for civilian and military lift. Since the 1990s, our policy has been to stockpile the Russian engine rather than develop a domestic engine. We are now reevaluating that policy, and you all have begun to give us a sense of how we should proceed.

In that context, I want to turn to General Shelton, who is known as someone who will give us frank, no-nonsense assessments, and we truly appreciate your contributions in leadership, General Shelton. I know you are going to retire soon. I am particularly glad you are going to stay in Colorado Springs, and I look forward to working with you whatever your retirement holds because I know you, and I know you are not really going to retire. Let me turn to you.

As the Commander of Air Force Space Command, you place a high value on mission assurance, given the critical importance of cost of the satellites that DOD launches. I have a multi-part question related to mission assurance.

Number one, can you explain what effects the launch failures in the 1990s had on DOD? That is number one.

Number two, can you explain the role of mission assurance in the current EELV program as compared to the late 1990s when those failures occurred?

Number three, finally, can you explain the importance of the added performance margin the Air Force puts on the EELV rockets and how that margin contributes to mission assurance?

General SHELTON. Thank you, Senator Udall. Thank you for your kind words too, of course.

Senator UDALL. Well deserved.

General SHELTON. As we look back at the 1990s, between 1997 and 1999, we had significant failures both on the military side and the commercial side, including three Titan IVs which launched our most significant payloads at that time.

We had adjusted our approach to mission assurance from what has been traditionally deep oversight into just insight. We pretty much gave it over to the contractors to provide their own mission assurance. We found out that just did not work well for us.

As we turned that around and went through some extensive introspection, had a nationally significant study come forward, we decided to get back into the deep oversight business, and that is what we do today. Very deep penetration of process, very deep penetration of actual processing of every launch vehicle. As I said in my opening statement, we treat every launch as if it is our very first, and so what happened in the past in terms of success, we do not pay much attention to. We pay a lot of attention to the launch of the day.

As we look at that performance margin, 7 percent, about 5 percent of that—5 of the 7 is for mission growth. We order launch vehicles about 2 years in advance. We see payloads sometimes get heavier during their development process toward the end, and we reserve that 5 percent. The additional 2 percent is just in case something goes wrong with that rocket. About a year and a half ago, we were launching a global positioning satellite (GPS) mission, and we had problems with the upper stage. Luckily, we had margin to make it to orbit or we would have had a failed mission. That is the reason for that margin. That is the reason for our continued emphasis on mission assurance.

Senator UDALL. In your opinion, do we need to develop a liquid rocket engine for medium and heavy lift, and if so, how urgent is that requirement?

General SHELTON. If you look at what has happened to us now in the last few months, I think it points to a vulnerability that we have. We had decided to rely on a foreign supplier. It is probably the most advanced rocket engine in the world, by the way. That has worked extremely well. If you look at the Atlas V performance, there is nothing to complain about the Atlas V performance.

But given that reliance, it is probably time to look at strategies for the future, and I think we can certainly help our liquid rocket engine industrial base by moving into such a program. I think we need to study the requirements. I think we need to look at what kinds of technologies we need to develop, but in my opinion, it is time to move off reliance on that foreign engine.

Senator UDALL. Thank you.

Senator NELSON. Senator Sessions?

Senator SESSIONS. Thank you. It is good to follow my chairman, Senator Udall.

To follow up on that, General Shelton, in your opinion is it a national security priority for the United States to develop an American-made engine that could replace the RD–180 first?

General SHELTON. Yes, sir. If you consider space a national security priority, then you absolutely have to consider assured access to space a national security priority. Given that we have a vulnerability here, it is time to close that hole.

Senator SESSIONS. I could not agree more. We definitely depend on space capability for communications, for observation, and it is just a base part of our national security, as well as our commercial activity.

Mr. Rogozin, a deputy prime minister in Russia, also said in May, "Russia is ready to continue deliveries of RD–180 engines to the United States only under the guarantee that they will not be used in the interest of the Pentagon." You are part of the Pentagon, are you not?

General SHELTON. Yes, sir.

Senator SESSIONS. Look, that is just not acceptable, and it puts us in a vulnerable position that I wish we did not have to be in, but it is time for us to rise to the occasion and fix this situation. I am open to ways to do it, and we will keep working to do it in a way that is effective.

But I have been pleased with the Senate legislation that we worked on. I think that balanced and considered the challenges that we faced and tried to do it in the right way. The House has also come up with a similar proposal. I am glad to have a public hearing about this and discuss it. Let us just keep talking about it to try to get it right.

Mr. Lightfoot, you have been at NASA for some time, and you started the National Institute for Rocket Propulsion Systems (NIRPS) and have studied these issues over the years. Does the institute at NASA have the people with the skills and experience that could assist the Air Force in this effort to develop an American replacement for this engine? I would ask, if so, would NASA desire to be compensated for their efforts?

Mr. LIGHTFOOT. Senator Sessions, I think the NIRPS that we put in place is not just NASA. DOD is part of that, as well as other agencies and a lot of the industry folks. I think the institute itself was set up to be able to pull together all the propulsion system resources this country has to solve problems that could come up, whatever they are. If we chose to go down that path, I surely would think we would use NIRPS. It would be part of that solution space, and you get to pull in the expertise that all the government agencies have if we choose to go that way.

That is not in our plan today. Of course, we would be interested in getting compensated for that. But I think the team right now works together fairly well with us and DOD from that standpoint.

Senator SESSIONS. You do have something, you believe, at NASA, and NASA has something they could contribute to the effort.

Mr. LIGHTFOOT. Yes. I think our expertise that has been hands-on for years in developing our own launch systems we can bring to that story as well.

The issue that Mr. Dumbacher talked about in terms of the lack of development of LOX/hydrocarbon engines in the past—this is a gap in our base, but the team at Marshall Space Flight Center, in particular, has been working on this for some time in a low level activity to try to keep up with that technology as we move forward. I think we can bring that to bear to help our friends out if we choose to go that way.

Senator SESSIONS. Mr. Dumbacher, I will ask you. You are more of an independent observer here perhaps, but do you think that there will be any fundamental technological engineering difficulties that would make it hard or unlikely that we could develop this engine? Or do you believe the United States could produce an engine similar to the RD–180 that could be as effective or more so?

Mr. DUMBACHER. Senator, I believe that we can do that, that we can develop an engine within a sufficient time and money. There are development risks associated with it, three in particular. One is the high pressure oxygen compatibility of the materials that we use in the engine system. Combustion stability has been an historic issue with large LOX/kerosene engines, and also how you handle the start transient depending upon which cycle you use for those engines. There are technical issues to be addressed. I think we can overcome those, but it is a matter of time and money required to do that.

Senator SESSIONS. Mr. Lightfoot, do you think it is also technologically—it seems to me it is a fairly mature technology now. How do you feel about it? What kind of confidence level do you have that such an engine could be produced?

Mr. LIGHTFOOT. Sir, I think that we could get to an engine, as Dan said. I think the challenge we have to look at is the launch system is not just the engine. There will be impacts that go to the launch vehicle, to the launch infrastructure. When we talk about a launch capability, I have an analogy I have been using related to—I have hybrid cars, 4-cylinder, 6-cylinder, 8-cylinder, and I have diesels. If I change your engine, I would probably change your car a little bit as well. We have to look at the impacts on not just building an engine and having an engine to use, but the impacts on the infrastructure that goes around that. Can we do it? I am sure we can with the right resources to go do it. But I think we have to make sure we understand the other pieces that come with that as we go forward.

Senator SESSIONS. My time is up.

Senator NELSON. Senator Cruz?

Senator CRUZ. Thank you, Mr. Chairman. Thank you, all of you, for coming here and providing your expertise.

In life, it is often a wise strategy to hope for the best and yet plan for the worst. That is especially true in the national security context. I would welcome the wisdom of this panel on what the implications would be for our national security if the worst occurs and what the best avenues we have to alleviate those implications.

In particular, General Shelton, I would like to start with you. Assume that conditions and relations with Russia deteriorate substantially. I hope that they do not, but assume that they do. Assume that Putin adopts a position of maximum belligerence and picks up the phone and instructs all engine exports to end tomorrow. What would the implications be for U.S. national security if that decision were made?

General SHELTON. Senator, as we look at that, as one of the number of scenarios we have considered, we think as a minimum that would be about $1.5 billion. We think that that would stretch out launches. We have to ramp up the production of our Delta factory, which would take some time. That would stretch out launches maybe 12 to 20 months in some cases; for the heavier missions, maybe even 48 months. That puts constellations at risk, and the ones that we are talking about, the heaviest ones, are our most significant constellations. It is dire. If that should happen, there is no question that inside this manifest that we are considering right now, there would be serious national security implications.

Senator CRUZ. To what extent could our existing stockpile of engines reasonably be stretched to cover the needs? How long could we expect it to cover our needs?

General SHELTON. Sir, we have 15 engines left right now. Depending on how we chose to meter those out, I think Mr. Lightfoot said in his opening statement that we would have to meet nationally to decide how we would allocate those engines. But that is all part of this set of scenarios that we are considering right now. We do not know the exact impact until we get together and decide how we would allocate those 15.

Senator CRUZ. On best case, are we talking a year? Are we talking 2 years? How long would you reasonably expect the stockpile to be able to meet the needs?

General SHELTON. We could meter that out over a number of years depending on what you decided to spend those engines on.

Senator CRUZ. Mr. Lightfoot, let me ask you the same hypothetical, maximum belligerence, but let us assume that Mr. Putin did not just say engine exports. He also said the Soyuz has a shutdown. No more Americans will have access to our launch capacity for manned launch. What would the impact be on the Space Station and on our needs?

Mr. LIGHTFOOT. I think we would clearly have to go assess what that would do to us from access to station. To date, we have seen no change in the behaviors at all. We continue to launch Soyuz and put people up there. I want to make sure that is really clear regardless of Rogozin's comments. Our teams are working together with the Russians very well to continue the ISS operations. Clearly the ISS is our stepping stone to our larger exploration program. We would have to go look at the implications associated with that, and it would be significant from that standpoint. Then we would work——

Senator CRUZ. Can you briefly describe, if it was cut off, what the implications would be in your best judgment?

Mr. LIGHTFOOT. Yes. We would want to accelerate our commercial crew activity so that we are launching from here, from the United States, from that standpoint, and let our partners that have bid on that proposal now and the one that we have in selection— let them come forward and show us how they would provide the access to the ISS that we need.

But it is more than just the launch to the station. The Russians also operate key components on the station just like we do for them. That would be the issues that we would have to go assess one by one.

Senator CRUZ. In light of those concerns, both with engines and manned launch capacity, if a decision were made to proceed forward with maximum speed towards acquiring the domestic capacity to fill these needs, realistically how quickly could we do so and how many commercial enterprises possess the skill and expertise to be credibly able to meet that need?

General SHELTON. I will start.

The only provider that is really in a serious certification process right now is SpaceX. If everything goes extremely well, a very green light schedule, by December of this year, we could have them certified. If you look at Atlas V, there are 10 configurations of Atlas V due to the various upper stages, strap-on solids, those sorts of things. SpaceX—there are seven of those 10 configurations that they could not launch. They do not have the lift capacity for that. They have a heavy vehicle planned in the future, but that is down the road a ways. That means that SpaceX could compete for some of those. We would need to ramp up Delta IV production to accommodate the rest. We are probably looking at, again, 12 to 48 months slip on some launches.

Senator CRUZ. Mr. Lightfoot, anything to add on the manned launch?

Mr. LIGHTFOOT. No. I think we would work with these guys to figure out which critical missions we needed to get done and how we would work them into the manifest. But we should expect a significant impact.

Senator CRUZ. How quickly could we fill the manifest?

Mr. LIGHTFOOT. At the current proposals that we have, we think we can be flying by 2017, putting humans into space from our location. I do not know if there is much we can accelerate at this point because of the way the process works, but what we would prefer to do is just keep the funding for the commercial crew program going so we can meet the 2017 date.

Senator CRUZ. Thank you very much.

Senator NELSON. Be prepared to answer the question, if you got more money, could you accelerate that to 2016.

Senator Wicker?

Senator WICKER. Why don't you just answer that question? [Laughter.]

Mr. LIGHTFOOT. I think part of the issue we are dealing with is, is we are in the middle of a procurement. Right? We have a procurement right now that we will make a selection on later this fiscal year. Having not seen the proposals because I am not part of that procurement board, I cannot tell you what the acceleration options are. However, at some point, when you order—we are in 2014 already here. When you order a rocket, we typically order them 3 years in advance from when we are doing it. That is where we are.

Senator WICKER. There are considerations other than funding that are going to take time.

Mr. LIGHTFOOT. Yes, sir. Yes, sir, exactly, to manufacture the long-lead items and all the different pieces that come into building these things.

Senator WICKER. I think probably the chairman would want you to get back to us about how we can be helpful in pushing the timeline.

Let me ask this. I will start with General Shelton and Mr. Estevez. Now, in developing the U.S. alternative to the Russian RD–180 engine, the Air Force research laboratories are going to want to be involved, and Stennis Space Center is going to be a key player. Can you tell us at this point how costs for testing compare between these two facilities? Given their respective workloads and priorities, would the developmental timeline and costs be less by utilizing the Stennis Space Center as opposed to the Air Force Research Laboratory (AFRL)?

General SHELTON. Sir, I could not give you an outright comparison, and I would not necessarily expect it would be an either/or. I would think that that would be divvied up. We have had work going on in the AFRL facility since 2007 on the hydrocarbon engine. That was part of the direction coming out after the decision to not co-produce RD–180s and to stockpile instead. I think Stennis has great capability. I think we would utilize Stennis for some things. I think we would use AFRL facilities for other things. We would use commercial facilities for yet other things.

Senator WICKER. Okay. Before we move to Mr. Estevez, you could go back, though, and get the committee some cost comparisons for testing in the past and supply them to us on the record. Would you be able to do that?

General SHELTON. Yes, sir.

Senator WICKER. Look for that and let us know.

General SHELTON. We will try to do something that is apples to apples. That may be difficult but we will give it a shot.

[The information referred to follows:]

The Air Force Research Lab (AFRL) Rocket Propulsion Division, located at Edwards Air Force Base, CA, has a mission to explore rocket propulsion science and technology for Air Force and Department of Defense applications. The primary mission of the National Aeronautics and Space Administration (NASA) Stennis Space Center (SSC), MS, is development testing, qualification testing, and production testing of engines. There are many variables in an engine test program and the types of testing and associated costs for both sites are nominally different; the AFRL focus is on experimentation and research, while the SSC focus is on testing and validation for acquisition activities. A specific test program is typically unique and tailored around a customer's test requirements. Thus, we have no comparable costs available between AFRL and SSC efforts.

While a comparison of test costs is not meaningful due to unique capabilities, we can provide updates on current efforts at both SSC and AFRL facilities. The Air Force is working jointly with NASA to conduct hot-fire testing of U.S.-designed hydrocarbon components in fiscal year 2017 using hardware from both NASA Marshall's Advanced Booster Engineering Demonstration and Risk Reduction (ABEDRR) hardware and AFRL's Hydrocarbon Boost (HCB) program. Planned development will leverage NASA's ABEDRR and AFRL's HCB to provide key engine component technical maturation and risk reduction. The Air Force intends to provide $3 million to the HCB effort in addition to the funding already allocated. The Air Force also plans to provide $37.6 million to NASA to complete the ABEDRR testing and modify the NASA Stennis Spaceflight Center test hardware.

Senator WICKER. Okay.

Mr. Estevez?

Mr. ESTEVEZ. First, I would reiterate what General Shelton said. But we are looking at this, how to move forward with a replacement for the RD–180, as a whole-of-government issue. To Mr. Lightfoot's earlier comments, we would look at NASA capabilities, as well as what we have inside DOD and, as General Shelton said, look at what the commercial sector is also doing. We have not decided what the best way forward is; ergo, it is preliminary to decide where we would start that development. We do want to move forward with some risk reduction activities. In fact, we put some money in the reprogramming action that we just put before Congress to do that.

Senator WICKER. Mr. Estevez, do you agree, though, with the General that Stennis and the AFRL would be key players in any path forward?

Mr. ESTEVEZ. I do.

Senator WICKER. Okay. Now, for all of you, who wants to volunteer here? GAO has argued that there is room for improvement in coordination between NASA and DOD for future programs. Who has seen this report, and what do you believe could be done to make the improvements that GAO has suggested would need to be made? Who wants to tackle that? Mr. Lightfoot?

Mr. LIGHTFOOT. I will start. Then I will let these guys jump in. We have done several things to——

Senator WICKER. Do they have a point?

Mr. LIGHTFOOT. I think when the report came out, they had a point. I think we have done a lot since then, though, to improve that communication.

Senator WICKER. Already?

Mr. LIGHTFOOT. Yes, sir. We both have folks on site at all of our new entrants and the ULA folks as well, and we share the information, as best we can, across with each other depending on where the certification process is between the launch vehicles. We are going through that process and sharing information, which we think is the most important thing as we move through certification of these new entrants in the process.

General SHELTON. Senator, I believe there is tremendous transparency between NASA and the Air Force. There are processes set up to ensure that we are communicating back and forth. There are summits that occur at NASA, Air Force, and the National Reconnaissance Office leadership levels. It is hard to imagine it could be any better. We have different requirements.

Senator WICKER. The GAO conclusion was perhaps a little unfair.

General SHELTON. Senator, that is not what I am saying. In the past, I would agree there were some areas we could do better in and we have.

Senator WICKER. Okay.

Mr. Estevez, let me ask you this. We are all agreed that there is a great opportunity for public/private partnerships in this engine development idea. Is that correct?

Mr. ESTEVEZ. Yes, sir. In fact, we are doing an assessment now about what course to take in a replacement for the RD–180. You can look at an inside-government-only development. That is probably not the best course, but we are going to look at that, look at jump starting some things, some risk reduction, and then turning that to the private sector, hopefully, that they will build. That is one way to do it. A public/private partnership is another way. We have an assessment, after the Mitchell study laid out some ways forward, that is ongoing inside the Air Force right now, and we expect that to come out sometime this fall.

Senator WICKER. General Mitchell, do you want to conclude my brief few seconds on that issue?

Mr. MITCHELL. Yes, sir. There are some risk reduction activities that need to bring the technology levels up in hydrocarbon engines that need to be invested in. That will take a year and a half or so or 2 years to bring those technologies up that were discussed. They have to do with the materials. They have to do with the modeling of the combustion instability and some of the piece parts of the engine itself, injectors and other components, that need to be matured over the next year-year and a half to position yourself to start a full-scale development program probably in the last fiscal year 2016–fiscal year 2017 timeframe.

Senator WICKER. Thank you, Mr. Chairman.

Senator NELSON. I am going to recess the committee momentarily to go over and finish the vote. Chairman Udall will take over the committee when he arrives.

Let me just ask. I have seen the Air Force study on a replacement for the RD–180. I have heard various estimates on costs. I have heard various estimates on time. Are we looking at, in reality, 7 or 8 years to have an engine ready to go in a rocket, whether it be a version of the Atlas V or whatever? Is that a realistic timeframe, or is it more or can it be less?

Mr. ESTEVEZ. Too soon to tell, 5 to 8 years is what we are looking at. We want to do this right, though, to the earlier discussion about mission assurance, and figuring out the course and what the most affordable way to do it is also a key part of that decision point. While this is a priority, there are other things in the mix. I would hesitate to make a firm projection at this point, Senator, until we know exactly where we are going. We do know we are going to replace it, though.

Senator NELSON. Do you want to give a ball park on cost to replace the RD–180?

Mr. ESTEVEZ. Estimates were in the $1 billion to $2 billion. Again, until we get a course ahead how we are going to do that public/private partnership, government-only, all those things change that dynamic. I would really hesitate to make a true assessment of that at this point.

Senator NELSON. That is overall cost, including the alterations to the rocket that you would put it in.

Mr. ESTEVEZ. I would have to go back and take that for the record, Senator, but I am happy to give you an estimate there.

[The information referred to follows:]

The $1 to $2 billion estimate is for an engine development program only. The additional cost associated with integrating a new engine into an existing launch vehicle can vary greatly depending on the designs involved. The cost associated will be significant, and could easily run into the hundreds of millions, if not more.

Senator NELSON. Okay.

The good news is that it seems like President Putin is not quite as aggressive as he first appeared to be. It is also fairly clear that Roscosmos certainly does not want to give up that income stream, and it looks like that from their standpoint, they clearly want to continue to supply the RD–180.

But we have seen this movie before. It was back a decade or so ago that we said we were going to start the process of the replacement of the RD–180, right when we started acquiring these in the 1990s, and then we backed off of that. Here we are again, and that is part of the issue of the day.

I am going to recess the committee because we are down to 1 minute to vote. I am going to see if I can sprint. The committee will stand in recess until the call of the chair. [Recess.]

Senator UDALL [presiding]. The committee will come to order. Thank you for your patience.

I want to recognize Senator Kaine for 5 minutes.

Senator KAINE. Thank you, Mr. Chairman, and thank you to the witnesses for your service and your testimony today.

I have questions that are primarily going to be addressed to General Shelton and Assistant Administrator Lightfoot on the Wallops facility in Virginia.

I guess it was last Sunday, July 13, Orbital successfully launched the second resupply mission to the ISS from Wallops in Virginia. Orbital is lined up to carry out eight cargo space missions to the ISS through 2016, making it a critical player in commercial space. Wallops is also in a unique position, and it is capable of launching certain national security payloads from that facility.

Administrator Lightfoot, what are some of the benefits of having facilities like Wallops for launching smaller and mid-size payloads?

Mr. LIGHTFOOT. Sir, I think you saw it today. The Cygnus spacecraft birthed to the ISS about 6:30 a.m. this morning. It was pretty exciting for us to get the crews there.

The other thing it gives us is it gives us two different access points to get to the station, not only two different providers in SpaceX and Orbital, but we now have two locations from which to fly, which helps us from that standpoint. It has been very good for us an agency to have the folks at Wallops and their little team do what they have done to provide us that access to the station.

Senator KAINE. Just on that, it is good to have two places to launch from. Is that just a matter of scheduling, gives you more flexibility or also are there aerospace reasons why launching sites in different parts of the country are helpful?

Mr. LIGHTFOOT. What it does is it gives the commercial providers—because we do not pick their launch site for them. It gives them the opportunity to get the best value for their launch vehicle, and so that is the advantage that they have had. We do not set where they fly from. They just go make that agreement themselves, and that makes it more of a competitive process.

Senator KAINE. What are we doing to ensure that national defense agencies have some redundant capability for launching national security payloads into space? In the event that problems at either Vandenberg or Canaveral would occur such as natural disasters, et cetera, I would imagine that redundancy is a positive. General Shelton?

General SHELTON. Senator, there are physics-based reasons for having two different launch locations. For example, going out of Vandenberg, you are looking at largely polar orbits or test activity that goes out to the west. From the Cape, you are looking at lower inclination orbits. There really is not a way to produce redundancy for that physics-based problem unless you build brand new launch facilities. So, yes, we would be susceptible to a very broad destructive kind of event, but that has not happened in the history of space flight.

Senator KAINE. Let me move on to the RD–180 replacement. General Shelton, you may have answered questions on this already. Forgive me for coming in a few minutes late. But what can DOD do to accelerate a timeline to develop a U.S.-built alternative to the Russian engine?

General SHELTON. Certainly it will take a very serious funding commitment, and we will go through some risk reduction efforts here and technology maturation efforts over the next couple of years. Then beyond that, it will take some very serious investment. If we want to stretch out the program, we can, but if we want to really get after a serious program, then we are going to have to have significant investment.

Senator KAINE. Thank you.

No other questions, Mr. Chairman. I just want to indicate that Wallops, the launch site in Virginia, is a well-kept secret. Most Virginians do not even know that rockets launch out of Wallops, which is just off the eastern shore, but more rockets have launched from Wallops than either Vandenberg or Cape Canaveral. The reason they are not generally known is that they are unmanned and they tend to be smaller, but it serves as a significant asset. We worked hard on it with our colleagues in Maryland because it is very close to the Maryland border. Chairman Mikulski has been a huge supporter of investments there. That additional launch capacity, I think, has served the Nation well, and I look forward to working with you in the future to continue that.

Thank you, Mr. Chairman.

Senator UDALL. Thank you, Senator Kaine. The Commonwealth never ceases to surprise all of us. [Laughter.]

I learned something as well. That is an important part of our whole aerospace consortium, if you will. Thank you for that.

Mr. Estevez, let me turn to you, if I might. Before the current 36-core block buy, we procured our space launch as a service using a commercial waiver under the Federal Acquisition Regulations (FAR) that provided no cost insight into the structure of the procurement. What was the result of this waiver on that particular decision?

Mr. ESTEVEZ. The statute requires us to acquire space launch services under FAR, part 12, which is a commercial service. There are good reasons for that, especially as we moved into commercial areas. However, we bought the block buy under FAR 15. We have full cost and pricing data from ULA. It gives us great insight into the cost structure of that. Going forward, I am not sure——

Senator UDALL. Would you recommend having the EELV program use it again?

Mr. ESTEVEZ. Again, we are looking at the benefits and the negatives on that. Certain commercial providers do not have to deal with the same business system background and the like that we require under FAR, part 15. It has to be weighed acquisition-by-acquisition, frankly. But there are benefits to having that full cost and pricing that have been helpful to us.

Senator UDALL. Let me follow up with asking you to give us an explanation. Can you explain the nature of the cost overruns of that prior EELV contract? Then, what cost savings were achieved in the current contract, and how were they obtained?

Mr. ESTEVEZ. The past was not really cost overruns because we were buying launch services as a contract-by-contract, launch-by-launch. We are buying a one each. But if you look at the program overall for the depth of the manifest, there was great cost growth; ergo, we ran into a Nunn-McCurdy situation for the EELV program.

What we were able to achieve by doing the 36-core buy is economies of scale. ULA could go to their industry subs and give them a deal because they know they are going to launch a certain number; ergo, it lowers the cost in total for that. It gave us price stability. It gave them an understanding of what their business base was going to be, $4.4 billion over our projections in fiscal year 2012 savings to DOD, to the American taxpayers. A great benefit to us.

Senator UDALL. Let me turn to Ms. Chaplain. Nice to see you, as always. I believe this is the third time you have testified this year before our subcommittee, which I believe qualifies you for frequent flyer status, whether on an airplane or rocket. You can maybe make the choice. [Laughter.]

Can you explain why the waiver under the FAR led to the lack of transparency in the cost increases in the EELV program?

Ms. CHAPLAIN. Yes. It is pretty simple. With the waiver, the government did not have the type of underlying cost and pricing data on critical pieces like the engines that it needed to make good negotiations, especially as it was going to commit to a large span of time under the block buy. Without that kind of data and if you are in a sole source environment, you are really crippled in terms of your negotiating position. If there is a competitive environment, it might not be such an issue because the competition itself can drive down prices.

Senator UDALL. You have reviewed the 36-core block buy, the current core block buy. Do you agree with that estimated cost savings of $4 billion on the current EELV contract?

Ms. CHAPLAIN. We have not thoroughly assessed the savings claim, but we do know that the Air Force took all the actions it needed to obtain those kinds of significant savings. They did gain much more insight into cost and pricing. They went through their launch processes, understood them more. They understood pieces of cost better and were just able to account for more things. When they went to the bargaining table, they were in a much better bargaining position.

Senator UDALL. General Mitchell, let me turn to you, if I might. Thank you for your service both on Active Duty but also on the committee that you helmed.

You recommended the development of a domestic engine, I believe, to replace the RD–180. I assume the committee reviewed proposals from industry. How mature are those proposals, and what are the major technical hurdles in their development?

Mr. MITCHELL. I think we talked to all of the folks who had engine developments, and they range from what I will call viewgraphs to some piece parts that have been done to concepts. Nobody has all of the technology ready to start a full-scale development program in our review. We think that that is going to take some investment and time to get the technologies up to where you could actually do what we call a full-scale development and commit to actually procuring the new engine.

Senator UDALL. It is more than possible, but there is a significant amount of time between here and there.

Mr. MITCHELL. Yes, sir. The areas primarily revolve around engine components, injectors, power heads, preverters, and then modeling and simulation of the combustion instability issue. We have better computers now of higher speed. They can better model those things but it takes some investment and algorithms to try and get a better handle on that. Combustion instability is a phenomenon that occurs in less than a second, and you cannot stop it. It will blow an engine up if it happens. The more you can do in computers, the less hardware you have to then have in your test program.

Senator UDALL. You have less than 1 second to get——

Mr. MITCHELL. Yes, sir, and you do not stop it. If it happens, it happens. You go get another engine.

Senator UDALL. Thank you for that insight.

Senator King?

Senator KING. Thank you, Mr. Chairman.

I want to go back and try to push down a little bit more on this RD–180 decision. I guess the first question—and perhaps, General Shelton, you are the best person to ask. If you are not, perhaps one of you all can chime in. Ms. Kim, you may be. How serious is the interruption risk? Is this a theoretical risk, or is there any indication of an interruption in supply by the Russians? General Shelton?

General SHELTON. Senator, I will echo what Mr. Lightfoot said earlier. We have seen no indication of an interruption threat other than what Mr. Rogozin said. We have seen no indication from the commercial side. We have talked to ULA extensively. They have talked to their counterparts in Russia extensively, and there has been no indication that that is a serious threat at this time.

Senator KING. Now, even after Ukraine, Crimea, the various unpleasantness, no threats.

General SHELTON. Yes, sir. Certainly the potential is still there, but what we are seeing right now is business as usual.

Senator KING. I want to press a little bit more on what it would mean. In answer to Senator Cruz's question, you have 15 of these motors in stock, in inventory in a sense. How many launches a year do we normally do? What do we have planned, say, for the next 5 years, total number of launches?

General SHELTON. We do roughly six or so a year of Atlas V, six, seven a year. That is how many engines you are going to burn every year.

Senator KING. Basically we have a 2-year backlog of inventory.

General SHELTON. We do.

Senator KING. There may not be a short answer to this, but clearly one of the other things we have to ask about is the cost implications of developing our own engine. That is not going to be free.

General SHELTON. No, sir. You have heard some projections here this morning, somewhere between $1 billion to $2 billion. The question then becomes can you stand not to pay that price or the potential of an interruption.

Senator KING. That is the question. My questions do not presuppose an outcome. I just want to be sure we are analyzing. This strikes me as a low-risk, high-consequence kind of situation. There is a low risk of this happening, but if it does happen, the consequences are high. Is that fair? Mr. Estevez, you nodded when I said that.

Mr. ESTEVEZ. That is fair. Again, the situation with Russia right now is volatile. So the risk is there. As General Shelton said, there is no indication that we would be cut off today. We can project into the future. Yes, there is a good rationale for why we would move down the path to develop our own engine. However, while we are doing that, use of the RD–180 is a cost-effective and proven way to launch our national security payloads.

Senator KING. There was another factor, as I understand, in the late 1990s when the decision was made to go with the RD–180, other than the fact that it appears to be a high quality, reliable engine, is—it is an odd thing to think about, but it was the desire to keep Russian rocket expertise in Russia. Are we not worried about that anymore, or is that no longer a factor? But that was apparently a national security consideration back when this decision was originally made.

General SHELTON. General Mitchell may want to comment more on this, but as I understand it, that was a consideration but certainly not the primary. If you look at this, this was really a commercial development as it started in the late 1990s. This was Lockheed-Martin building their own rocket, and they chose the RD–180 engine.

Mr. MITCHELL. I will just add to that, that the conversations on the RD–180 actually started with General Dynamics before they were procured by Lockheed-Martin. The Russians came to General Dynamics and said for $100,000 we can go modify the RD–171 engine which flies on the Zenit and produce you an engine that will be able to fit under your rocket. It was a deal they could not pass up. It was driven by a political situation but enabled by the cost benefit of doing it, and then the initial engines were only $10 million apiece. That cost has gone up, but initially it was very financially attractive to do it.

Senator KING. That is the kind of analysis that we have to do today. Clearly in an ideal world, we would want to make our own engines and have control of that piece of the industrial base. On the other hand, this is a proven quality product, and there will be additional costs.

By the way, who makes this decision? Does Congress make this decision? Does the Air Force make it? Does ULA? Who is going to decide when to move from the RD–180 to another engine?

General SHELTON. Sir, I would speculate that what would happen here is the executive branch would bring a proposal to Congress and then Congress ultimately has to decide whether or not to spend the money.

Senator KING. You see it as part of the appropriations process, in effect.

General SHELTON. Absolutely, sir.

Senator KING. I realize, Mr. Chairman, my time is expiring, but I would like to ask one more question.

A totally different subject—I notice the purchase and the competition versus single source. Under the proposed rules for 2015 and 2016, there were going to be 14 competitive cores and 20 only ULA-capable. Under the President's budget for 2015, it is 7 competitive cores and 20 ULA cores. It just strikes me—those 20 were inviolate? The competitive part got cut in half. The other got cut zero. Talk to me about that decision.

General SHELTON. It actually is a very involved answer. Many of those launches that were set aside for competition were GPS launches. As we looked at the health of the GPS constellation and we have decided that those are projected to live longer than expected, we did not need to procure the GPS launches on the schedule that we thought we needed to. We have stretched that program out. That resulted in the loss of five of those seven that are no longer available for competition.

Another launch became too heavy, such that nobody but ULA could lift it.

Another launch was taken out for requirements reasons, and because we had a 36-core commitment to ULA as part of our pricing arrangement, we had to plug that hole that we had created by taking one of the requirements out. That results in the seven.

It really was not an anticompetitive thing, and as we said all along, it was up to 2014. It is seven now. We think we may get an eighth in fiscal year 2015. But that is where we stand, and that is the reason we have reduced the number available for competition.

Senator KING. Just as we were talking about how the Russian engine creates risks, I think having a sole supplier creates risks for the country, not necessarily national security risks, but certainly financial risks. I believe that we need to move toward competition as rapidly and efficiently as possible just from the common sense competition is better than monopoly approach.

General SHELTON. Yes, sir, we would absolutely agree with you. The advantage we have with the current provider—it is a firm, fixed price arrangement. We know exactly what the costs are.

Senator KING. Thank you.

Mr. ESTEVEZ. If I could, Senator. DOD's position in working with the Air Force is to drive you that competition, and that is what we put in the program when we moved to both the block buy to decrease the cost and at the same time drove to competition. The fact that the manifest moves around for budgetary and because of the health of the constellation reasons, it is not picking on those. It just happens to be that those are the ones——

Senator KING. You understand how it would appear.

Mr. ESTEVEZ. I absolutely do understand that. But I want to just reemphasize that we are committed to driving down that competition road to do this.

Senator KING. I understand block buys are better than one off and you get a better price, and you have gotten that better price. But I think as a general principle, competition is where we ought to be heading.

Thank you.

Senator UDALL. Thank you, Senator King.

General Shelton, let me turn to you again. The EELV program mates its payload in a vertical configuration. Can you explain why that is done in terms of cost and risk?

General SHELTON. Yes, sir. We had to standardize how we were going to do this across our fleet. It has to do with really fragile satellites, how they are manufactured, how the lifting mechanisms work, all that. We standardize to vertical. You basically take a payload out, encapsulate it in its payload faring. We lift it up vertically and set it down on top of the launch vehicle. That has become our standard practice, and there are lots of good engineering reasons for doing it that way.

Senator UDALL. Let me turn to the Atlas V. It has a proven track record. We also agreed that we want more competition, and Senator King's got to the specifics on the competitive side versus the block buy side. But would you agree that we need a tested and certified domestic alternative that meets all relevant performance criteria before we halt the use of the current engine?

General SHELTON. Senator, if we can continue to purchase RD–180s, that is the most economical approach. No doubt about it. If we got into a situation where that supply was interrupted and we had to go into some sort of crash program on development of an engine, that is a wholly different matter. My personal opinion, if we can continue to buy RD–180s, we ought to buy them. It is a good deal.

Senator UDALL. What resources are being utilized on the part of the Air Force to help SpaceX become certified for DOD launches? When do we expect that process to be completed?

General SHELTON. Senator, we are spending 136 people on the problem and probably through fiscal year 2014, it will be somewhere around $60 million, probably approaching $100 million by the time we are done. As I said earlier, if we can accomplish this on what we would consider to be a very green light schedule, they will be certified by December. As we look at what we are projecting with a higher confidence on the schedule, we think it is going to be the first quarter of calendar year 2015.

Senator UDALL. I have one last question. Let me restate my previous question. I am not sure you answered it in the way I was hoping—not the actual answer but just that you heard what I was asking.

Given the proven track record of Atlas V and the importance of competition in the launch market, would you agree that we need a tested and certified domestic alternative that meets all relevant performance criteria before we halt the use of the current engine? I think you said yes, but I want to make sure I was clear on that.

General SHELTON. I did say yes, Senator, because if you look at the manifest, Atlas V lifts about two-thirds of our manifest.

Senator UDALL. Thank you. I am going to yield to Senator Nelson.

Senator NELSON [presiding]. I will still do cleanup.

Senator Cruz?

Senator CRUZ. Thank you, Mr. Chairman.

I would like to follow up on some of the very good questions that Senator King asked focusing on competition. General Shelton, how would you describe the benefits of competition in terms of acquiring engines and the capabilities for launch?

General SHELTON. Senator, I think there is no question that competition brings lower prices. It brings innovation and new ideas. What it cannot substitute for yet is reliability. We have a proven performer here, in fact, two lines, Delta and Atlas, that are very proven performers. The question we have to answer is, can we get to the place where we are as comfortable with a new entrant as we are with our current provider? That is why we have a very rigorous detailed certification process that is engineering-based, has 19 different engineering review boards that we will work our way through. That will have to be the substitute for numbers of launches. 72 in a row is a pretty good track record.

Senator CRUZ. When do you expect it is possible for all of these contracts to be competitively bid?

General SHELTON. Our schedule right now says that starting in fiscal year 2018, it will be a full and open competition.

Senator CRUZ. Between now and then, what is reasonable to expect?

General SHELTON. Between now and then, we have the 36-core buy with ULA. We will have at least seven, maybe eight launches available for competition, and there may be—who knows—some pop-up opportunities along the way as well. But we have a contractual agreement for a 36-core buy with ULA right now.

Senator CRUZ. Am I right in assuming that even with a competitive bid, it is entirely possible the current provider would win that bid?

General SHELTON. Absolutely.

Senator CRUZ. But with the benefits of competition, the taxpayers may get a far more favorable price through vigorous competition than they would with a no-bid contract.

General SHELTON. Pencils will be sharpened. Yes, sir.

Senator CRUZ. I would encourage expediting efforts down that road.

Mr. Estevez, you said a moment ago, if I heard you correctly, that what had been discussed here was a good rationale why we would go down the path towards development of a new engine. I want to understand that comment and reconcile it with the administration's statement of administration policy on June 17th where the administration objected to the House allocating funds to a new engine. Can you explain in your judgment what we should be doing towards developing a domestic engine so that we are not dependent upon Russian providers?

Mr. ESTEVEZ. There are a number of different paths that we can take to develop a new engine. What we said for that $220 million, I believe it was, is it is preliminary to be putting that money into the budget within the trade space of the budget at this point where we do not know the course that we are going to take to pursue development of a new engine.

Now, we have just asked for some reprogramming to do some risk reduction, and there is probably, as General Mitchell alluded to earlier, some time that you need to do that risk reduction before we decide whether it is going to be a public/private partnership that develops it, we will go to a commercial entity that will develop engines based our risk reduction, or it is inside the government process to do that. It is not that we do not want to go down the path in getting a new engine. It is the fact that the money was preliminary for where we are in that direction.

Senator CRUZ. What is your best case estimate for design, construction, test, and certification of a new engine both in terms of cost and time?

Mr. ESTEVEZ. Again, that will depend on the course that we select on getting to a new engine.

Senator CRUZ. But give me the best case.

Mr. ESTEVEZ. Eight years.

Senator CRUZ. Eight years. We talked earlier that if Russia cuts off these exports tomorrow, we do not have 8 years' worth of engines sitting in the warehouse. Is that right?

Mr. ESTEVEZ. That is correct.

Senator CRUZ. If the ramp-up to develop a new engine is substantially longer than our capacity to survive not having these imports, it would seem there is some considerable exigency to starting that process now and not getting caught flat-footed if the worst comes to pass.

Mr. ESTEVEZ. Of course, if that happened, if we were cut off, we would use the stock that we have and we would allocate those in an interagency process. We would ramp up production of Delta, which can launch our manifest. As General Shelton said earlier, it would cause some significant delay and put some risk into our constellations, but we would do that. Commercial providers that we are pushing for our competitive environment will come on board. They will be able to launch some of the manifest, so there are mitigations. Now, those things will cost us money, and they will, as I said, put some risk into the time we get some of those constellations up.

In the meantime, I would say throwing money at a problem that we do not know where we are going is not a good idea either at this point. It is not just a matter of rushing money into a development of a new engine. We want to do that in a considered manner so we get the engine that we need.

Senator CRUZ. Although if you said it is 8 years, the longer we delay the beginning of that 8 years, the further out the end of that 8 years is.

Dr. Kim, do you have any thoughts on this question? We would welcome your thoughts as well.

Dr. KIM. Our study did not look to an independent schedule estimate assessment, so I cannot comment on that.

Senator CRUZ. Thank you very much.

Senator NELSON. Of course, were the worst to happen, that it cut off today, in addition to the Delta heavy to launch the heavy payloads, assuming that SpaceX is certified by the end of the year, you would have that capability of launching medium-sized payloads. All is not lost were he to do the unlikely thing of shut off Roscosmos.

Senator Sessions?

Senator SESSIONS. Thank you.

I went past the Pentagon the other day, and we discussed once again—did they actually build this thing in 1 year? Mr. Estevez, this delay costs more. Here DOD has asked for $40 million for technology reduction for commercial new engine development this fiscal year through reprogramming. It will be needed to develop strategies. We ought to have a strategy by now. How long does it take to develop a strategy? Initiate engine risk reduction efforts, technology maturation activities, early concept studies, and surveys. It goes on to focus on key risk components, technological development.

I would just say if this were a private business and they got a major supplier that they no longer find reliable, they would get busy right now. Why can we not develop a situation now?

Now, I understand DOD is predicting, Mr. Chairman, it might cost $2 billion to develop the engine. I have heard recently that one of the people who would be wanting to supply it said they could do it for $840 million and would do it within 4 years and would put penalties on themselves if they did not produce that.

Mr. Estevez, do you think that is possible? Why do we not get busy? The fundamental question is are we going to continue with the Russian engine. Have we made a decision not to? If we are not going to do so, which I think we have no choice but to make that decision, why do we not get busy and get this done and not drag it out?

Mr. ESTEVEZ. We agree that we should be moving away from the Russian engine. We want to use the Russian engine while it is available while we go through that development effort. Without sounding glib, it is rocket science and the development of new engine integration of that. If there is a commercial company that is willing to go do that, we are happy to work with that, and that is one of the options that we are looking at is whether we can do this in the commercial sector, how much government support is going to be needed. You have read our reprogramming action.

Senator SESSIONS. How many years do you project this to take?

Mr. ESTEVEZ. Our estimates are 5 to 8, Senator.

Senator SESSIONS. Five?

Mr. ESTEVEZ. Five to 8 years.

Senator SESSIONS. That is not acceptable.

Ms. Chaplain, do you think it is going to take 5—you mean to actually have the engine produced.

Mr. ESTEVEZ. Have the engine developed.

Senator SESSIONS. How long will it take us to decide on what process we need, what kind of engine, and get moving on it?

Mr. ESTEVEZ. The Air Force is conducting an assessment right now that will be ready in the September timeframe what we believe our best, most affordable course within the timeframe on development is. Again, that will look at public/private partnership, internal government, or a commercial outsource on that.

Senator SESSIONS. General Shelton, you know the history of this better than anyone. Do you agree that if we keep dragging this out, there is a danger we will slip back into uncertainty and delay, delay, costs go up, and maybe nothing ever gets done?

General SHELTON. That is a concern, Senator.

Senator SESSIONS. You have been at this for a long time. You are about to leave DOD. Share with me what you think. Is there a danger and what do you think about it?

General SHELTON. We can stretch things out. We can make it longer.

Senator SESSIONS. Unwisely you mean.

General SHELTON. Absolutely.

Senator SESSIONS. Ms. Chaplain, do you have any thoughts? You have been around these programs for a long time yourself, and I think even some of your recommendations were taken into account, as you noted, saved $4 billion on the procurement that we have now, which was a good step. Do you have any idea how we could move quicker and less expensively in this crisis?

Ms. CHAPLAIN. I have been around long enough not to trust the numbers being thrown around today on either side and by vendors.

Senator SESSIONS. You could put a penalty on a vendor.

Ms. CHAPLAIN. Yes, but sometimes you get stuck and when the problems happen, you go back to a cost-plus arrangement which the government has done numerous times during the middle.

We do not know what we are actually pursuing right now. Is it a replacement, what is the design going to be? Is it going to extend all the way into the design of a whole launch vehicle? The more extensive it gets, the longer it takes. I agree that the need might be compelling, and if we lose time, we will be rushing activities even more later. The more you compress and have to take on a lot of concurrency in your acquisition program to meet tight deadlines, the more you are at risk of having problems later on. It is important to, first, figure out what it is we are really doing, get a good plan, and have disciplined processes in place. But I agree that if it is going to happen, we need to start working soon.

Senator SESSIONS. Thank you all. It was a good panel. It is an important issue.

General Mitchell, do you have any thoughts on this?

Mr. MITCHELL. Yes, sir. Just as one data point, when we were doing the EELV program, the RS–68 engine, which flies on the Delta, was a new development in a competitive environment. It took the contractor 6 years and $1 billion to develop that engine. That was without government oversight at the time. That was straight commercial in the competitive environment where Boeing was competing with Lockheed-Marin, and it took them 6 years and $1 billion in 2013 dollars to do it. That is a data point for you. They were trying to be as aggressive as they could because they were in a competitive environment, and it was commercially developed.

Senator SESSIONS. I just do not understand that.

Mr. MITCHELL. But that is a point for you.

Senator SESSIONS. My time is up.

But the plan was to develop an engine and many of the similar technologies in the Russian engine, nothing particularly new. If we got busy on it, I think we would save money in the long run. The longer we delay it, the more alternatives we are going to have to use, more expensive launches, delaying of launches, and all that. I just wish we could go faster and make a decision.

Mr. Chairman, I am glad you are chairing this. Having flown on rockets and come back to be with us, it is not an issue that you do not know a lot about. You know a lot about it, and I appreciate you and Senator Udall for having the hearing.

Senator NELSON. My critics wish that I had gone on a one-way trip. [Laughter.]

Senator SESSIONS. I have to tell this story. I was debating. I thought my opponent had said something against NASA, and I said I think we should explore the solar system and go to Mars, that I would like to go to Mars. He jumped up and reached in his pocket and said I will be the first to contribute to sending you to Mars. I thought that was the highlight of his campaign. [Laughter.]

Senator NELSON. He only got about 5 percent of the vote.

This is rocket science. Therefore it is not easy and these decisions are not easy. Ms. Chaplain has the historical perspective that somehow the cost of these programs grow, but they especially grow when you realize you are not just developing an engine. You are integrating it into a launch vehicle. You are going through a certification process, and then you have to have the ground systems infrastructure. Does that add cost, Ms. Chaplain?

Ms. CHAPLAIN. Yes, it certainly does, and I do not believe that is all being brought into the mix at this point with the numbers we are hearing about.

Senator NELSON. What do you think about it, Mr. Dumbacher?

Mr. DUMBACHER. I think, as you pointed out, Senator, this is a major, complex systems issue. It is not just an engine itself. We have technical issues we have to work out for a LOX/kerosene engine, but we also have to figure out how to integrate that into a launch vehicle. Typically when we develop engines, they are very integrally tied to the launch vehicle that we put them in. You cannot just move one engine from one launch vehicle to another very simply. You have to go through the entire systems process, the ground systems, the logistics, and take into account all the complex technical interactions that you have to deal with in a design that is trying to go from 0 to 17,000 miles an hour in the space of a few minutes. It is a very complex systems approach. It has affect on the industrial base, and decisions that are made on one launch system affect other launch systems.

It reaches across the government. We know that if there is a major decision made with the NASA solid propulsion base, it affects the Navy's strategic D–5 missile program. We also know that if changes are made in terms of flight rate for the RS–68 and the Delta 4s, that has impact over on the RS–25 usage and costs for the SLS. We have to look at this access to space question from an overall systems perspective and account for all of the complexities that are in this, not just the engine itself. The engine is one key part of it, but there are larger other impacts that have to be addressed.

Senator NELSON. Plus, once you have the new engine in the new rocket, then you have to do payload integration, and that takes time and money in the new vehicle.

Senator King, you had a question.

Senator KING. Senator, you mentioned this was a record-breaking hearing, and it is for me because it is the longest SASC hearing that I have been to where the word "sequester" has not been mentioned. [Laughter.]

I want to ask that question. I noticed the President's budget is listed as your planning budget, but the President's budget, as I recall, does not include the sequester. Does the sequester affect your procurement decisions, or are these forward procured, already contracted, and we do not worry about the sequester at least as far as these 36 cores are concerned, General?

General SHELTON. Senator, if sequestration comes back in 2016, which is the law, we would have all kinds of priority decisions to make across DOD. What we have right now are pricing agreements with ULA on that 36 cores. We do not have actual procurements. Those are done in that given fiscal year. Come fiscal year 2016, the buys that would be included in that fiscal year would be considered for whether or not those were priorities for DOD.

Senator KING. That is one of the charming effects of the sequester. It not only messes up budget planning, but it also could end up costing us money because we broke the 36 procurement block. We would end up paying more. Is that correct?

General SHELTON. That would be a negotiation with ULA, but I think the answer to that would be very likely yes.

Senator KING. The short answer is that sequester would affect what we are talking about here today, whether it is planning for a new engine or the launches or the acquisition of various launch vehicles. Sequester is a factor in everything that we have been discussing. Is that correct?

General SHELTON. Yes, sir.

Senator KING. Thank you.

Senator NELSON. In other words, sequester is going to have an impact on assured U.S. access to space.

Let me do some cleanup here, and then you all jump in if you have any more.

Mr. Lightfoot, NASA is flying on SpaceX right now, going to and from cargo to the station. All right. Now, General Shelton, you said that with it is going to take an aggressive effort in order to get SpaceX certified to fly DOD missions. What is the additional certification required to meet your certification needs that NASA has not already certified?

General SHELTON. I will let Mr. Lightfoot talk about his side of this, but NASA has not certified SpaceX for their, for example, interplanetary missions. They are carrying cargo back and forth to the station, but in terms of the really high priority science missions, they have not certified SpaceX.

Mr. LIGHTFOOT. I think that is an important point. Just to frame it up here, there are classes of missions, and those classes range from A to D. This is simple stuff. But then there is a category of launch vehicles as well, and they are 1 to 3, 1 being the ones that we would take the most risk on, 3 being the ones that we would fly our most important payloads on.

Senator NELSON. Namely humans.

Mr. LIGHTFOOT. Yes, sir.

What we have done is the missions that we are flying to the ISS with Orbital and SpaceX, the cargo is considered class D, which is the least level—where we are willing to take the most risk as an agency. What we did is we did not do as much insight into that from a launch vehicle perspective as we would, say, on a class A mission.

However, what is really important is we focused most of our real oversight when they get close to the ISS because that is when critical activities can occur. The activity associated with the birthing today of the Orbital Cygnus and the SpaceX Dragon—those we made them do a series of tests, a series of approaches, back-outs, all these things we do to ensure our own safety. Really what you are talking about is a risk categorization here in terms of the type of mission or spacecraft you are flying and the launch vehicle that it goes on.

For us, we are working on a Jason 3 flight that will be in December 2015. SpaceX is not certified for that flight yet. We are working through the certification process with them on that one, just like the Air Force is on the missions that they need. We have them flying to the ISS, SpaceX and Orbital, but the certification for the next class of payload is the thing we are working on. Then there will be an even further certification, as you said, for when we have a commercial group provider as well.

Senator NELSON. Anybody want to add to that? [No response.]

Secretary Estevez, what about the cost of accelerating a new entrant certification compared to developing a new engine?

Mr. ESTEVEZ. Based on the costs of what we are doing now, obviously it is much cheaper to have a commercial provider, a capable, certified commercial provider, who can launch our payloads than it would be to develop a new engine. Now, right now we are not in a place where the providers that we have as new entrants can put up rockets that can launch the full manifest of payloads that are going on the Atlas 5.

Senator NELSON. You could with the Delta 4.

Mr. ESTEVEZ. I could with the Delta 4.

Senator NELSON. But that is going to cost some more.

Mr. ESTEVEZ. Yes, absolutely true. Development of a new engine and the integration costs of that are obviously much more expensive than the cost that it costs us to certify the new entrant. But, again, I want to make sure that we are certifying new entrants that are capable of launching the payloads that we are launching. Otherwise, I will be sitting up here and General Shelton's successor about why we launched into the ocean, and I do not want to be doing that either.

Senator NELSON. Mr. Dumbacher, have we missed any other potential options other than a new launch vehicle or engine development that could address this RD–180 potential problem?

Mr. DUMBACHER. I think you have seen, Senator, across the board from DOD and NASA the involvement with General Mitchell's study and what it would take to replace the RD–180. That was all good work and I do not need to refute or take on any of that.

I think, again, back to your previous question, I think my caution would be that we make sure we address this from an overall systems perspective and a larger perspective than just an engine replacement because it does have ramifications to other launch systems. These decisions are long-term and have ramifications for lots of years. The decision that this country made at the end of the Apollo program to dramatically reduce our work on LOX/hydrocarbon engines is still playing out today and is part of this conversation that we are having this morning. I think we need to be aware of that, that these decisions are long-ranging, have large impacts, and the unintended consequences that can be had with any of these decisions we need to think carefully through to make sure that we do not inadvertently end up in a place we do not want to be as a country.

Senator NELSON. Just to make it more complicated, for example, you have already mentioned the impact on the Navy's rockets, which are solid rockets. If you do not have a solid rocket program in the other departments, that means the cost to the Navy is going to go up.

Mr. DUMBACHER. That is correct. In the past, NASA has worked with the Department of the Navy in the strategic missile program on what the impacts would be to them from an industrial base perspective and a supply chain perspective if NASA were to do something different than the solids. We understand that. NASA understands what that industrial base implication is, and we have to be wary of that.

We also, as I mentioned earlier, need to be aware of the ramifications and the impacts on the liquid booster side between RS–68 and the supply chain that is shared between the RS–68 and the RS–25.

In the end, I think our problem has been—in my view, the issue is getting the cost down and what we need to do to get the cost down. This Nation has spent over the last 40 years making significant investments in LOX/hydrogen, solid propulsion expertise. We are the world leaders in that, and I think it behooves us to look at those possible solutions as part of the overall system implications.

Senator NELSON. Can anybody on the panel give us the historical perspective of how many programs we have actually started and then canceled and how this plays into this decision? How can we ensure that if we start this new program which, as I mentioned at the outset, some of us on the SASC have put $100 million in this coming fiscal year to start it—how can we be assured that this is not going to get canceled in a few years and therefore the waste of the money?

Mr. ESTEVEZ. I cannot give you the number, Senator, of how many programs—I am sure we could get you that—over the course of time. From an acquisition perspective, one of the things that we are trying to accomplish under Better Buying Power is do not start programs unless you are going to fund them and you are going to put the right structure in place to follow through on those programs. On the development side, there is always going to be some growth, especially in a high risk program like this that is complex. But we would have to commit the dollars in the budget. Again, that goes back to my earlier things of how are we going to do this and we are not sure what the course would be to develop a replacement whether it is commercial sector or public/private partnership and the whole integration of that for the RD–180.

[The information referred to follows:]

Upon review, since the mid-1990s, the Department of Defense (DOD) has not taken a rocket engine development program to a milestone decision and then subsequently cancelled it. DOD has had a number of engine science and technology activities during that period but none were elevated to a development program with the expectation that an operational rocket engine would be developed and fielded as a result.

Mr. ESTEVEZ. I will go to Senator King's point on sequestration. Of course, that also impacts the point on the budget and where that trade space is related to this.

Senator NELSON. Senator McCain?

Senator MCCAIN. Thank you, Mr. Chairman. I thank the witnesses.

General Shelton, you are widely quoted as saying generally the person you are going to do business with you do not sue. Do you stand by that statement?

General SHELTON. Senator, the context for that was the conversation on the litigation between SpaceX and the Air Force, and yes, I do stand by that statement. We are trying very hard to get them certified and spending a lot of money, a lot of people.

Senator MCCAIN. First of all, what about the fact that already there is a suit pending by the ULA subsidiary seeking $400 million in additional payments from the Air Force? In other words, if some company or corporation thinks that they are not being fairly treated, you do not think that they should be able to sue? That is not our system of government, General Shelton. I do not really get your statement except that it shows real bias against the ability of any company or corporation in America to do what they think is best for their company or corporation. A subsidiary of ULA is suing for $400 million. Do you think they should be suing?

General SHELTON. Senator, that is over a technical payment situation.

Senator MCCAIN. Oh, I see. It is okay it is over a technical payment situation but not any other. General Shelton, you have really diminished your stature with this committee when you decide whether people or organizations or companies should be able to sue or not and make comments about them.

Ms. Chaplain, it seemed all of a sudden that the Air Force now found out that GPS satellites would now be able to stay up longer. Was that not known for a long time?

Ms. CHAPLAIN. They do analyses of the constellation on a regular basis and see how they are going to last. They tend to make adjustments to the manifest based on that. It is just not unusual to see changes, though the ones that were made this year were a little more substantial than usual.

Senator MCCAIN. The decision to cut the competitive launches even more by delaying launches really should not have come as a surprise.

Ms. CHAPLAIN. It is never a surprise to me generically that there are changes to the manifest either based on budgetary reasons or the length of a constellation. I have never believed you should trust what that manifest is year to year.

Senator MCCAIN. Facts are stubborn things.

Mr. Kendall, who we had extensive conversations with when he came up in the SASC for his job because of the failure—is it not true that ULA has breached Nunn-McCurdy more than once or twice? Is that true, Ms. Chaplain?

Ms. CHAPLAIN. At least the last one that I know of was the most recent one. There may have been one before that.

Senator MCCAIN. At least we know of one breach of Nunn-McCurdy, which is cost overruns of a dramatic and significant amount. That did not seem to bother anybody in the Air Force or the industrial complex because now, instead of increasing the numbers of competitive launches, we have decreased the competitive launches to an outfit that breached Nunn-McCurdy because of cost overruns. How does that give them any credibility? Do you want to respond to that? You do not have to.

Now, Mr. Estevez, we will now see a total of three, although perhaps Congress will mandate at least one additional competitive launch, and that is fine with you. Is that right?

Mr. ESTEVEZ. Senator, we are committed to the competitive course. We are aggressively pursuing to get SpaceX certified so that they can launch our satellites. They do not have the capability based on their current certification process to launch the full manifest of those satellites, but we look forward to getting them to be able to launch the ones that they are capable of launching.

Senator MCCAIN. Even though they have just completed a third successful launch. Is that right?

Mr. ESTEVEZ. That does not complete the certification process, Senator.

Senator MCCAIN. I know that. But the certification was supposed to take place in January. Is that correct?

Mr. ESTEVEZ. They are on their path to certification. It was not supposed to be completely certified in January to my knowledge.

Senator MCCAIN. Do you know when you will make a final decision?

Mr. ESTEVEZ. As General Shelton discussed earlier, if everything goes well with their certification process, they should be certified by the end of this year.

Senator MCCAIN. Mr. Lightfoot, NASA introduced launch competition into its processes by having two competing companies for the commercial audit transportation service contract. Have there been benefits of that, Mr. Lightfoot?

Mr. LIGHTFOOT. Yes, sir, we think we have gotten a good value in the process. The payloads we are launching are what we call class D because we have the two providers to get to the ISS.

Senator MCCAIN. Let us talk about the so-called great savings that is supposed to take place with a block. You saved—quote, saved—you are arguing, General Shelton, that the Air Force repeatedly said it has saved $4.4 billion on space launch costs by awarding a sole source block buy contract to ULA, disregarding the fact that ULA breached Nunn-McCurdy, which required the notification to Congress of cost overruns. But it is really cost avoidance.

Ms. Chaplain, do you have a view on that of whether that is actually a, quote, saving of the $4 billion which was advertised because of the sole source block buy contract to ULA?

Ms. CHAPLAIN. What it represents is—the ultimate price that they negotiated was substantially lower than the price they started out with in the negotiations. We did not investigate the exact $4.4 billion and what was behind it, but we do know that the Air Force took a number of actions to arm themselves with better information for the negotiation process, principally getting more information on costs and pricing in preparation.

Senator MCCAIN. Actually, the Office of Management and Budget refers to cost savings as a reduction in actual expenditures. That has not occurred in the EELV program.

I think, Mr. Chairman, that the issue of Russian rockets has been already pretty well massaged, but the fact is we are seeing here—and I do not predict, but a few years ago, there was a situation concerning the Air Force tanker. I did not like it at the time and I fought against it at the time. People went to jail and people were fired. I do not like this deal. I do not like the fact that we are now going to have basically maybe three—or if Congress has its way, four—competitive space launches given to an outfit that has breached the cost overruns to the degree that it required notification to Congress of cost overruns.

I thank you, Mr. Chairman.

Senator NELSON. Thank you, Senator McCain.

When you look at the value of competition, it is clearly well established. For example, NASA is going through a competition now of human rating rockets to take astronauts to and from the ISS, and there are probably at least three competitors in that competition.

Senator MCCAIN. What we are seeing here, Mr. Chairman, is a reduction in planned competition for whatever reasons. The actual reality is, despite Mr. Kendall's admonition to increase competition, we are seeing a decrease in competition. Then when the company does not like it and goes to court, they are criticized by a uniformed officer who really has no business talking about the conduct of a corporation as to what their legal options are.

Senator NELSON. The Russians have certainly brought this to a head. At the outset of the hearing, it was mentioned that it was the policy of the U.S. Government back in the 1990s, once we decided to buy the RD–180 from the Russians because it is an excellent engine and it was cheaper and we were employing Russian engineers and scientists instead of them going elsewhere on the planet—but it was the policy of the government at the time we were going to develop a follow-on engine. That got put aside. We are where we are particularly because of the deputy prime minister's sarcastic comments from Russia even though the statements were said—he made them at the time—he was only going to not supply the RD–180 for military launches. He is still going to provide them for civilian. But you will notice there was not a peep out of Roscosmos. They obviously want to continue that.

Nevertheless, it brings it to a head, and it brings us to the table today. These are complicated decisions, multifaceted, involving many different programs, but all of which come down to the bottom line, assured access to space for the United States.

We want to thank you all. You have been most enlightening.

The hearing is adjourned.

[Whereupon, at 11:43 a.m., the subcommittee adjourned.]

[Questions for the record with answers supplied follow:]

QUESTIONS SUBMITTED BY SENATOR MARK UDALL

RD–180 FOREIGN SUPPLIER

1. Senator UDALL. General Shelton, would you please walk me through the history of how U.S. rockets ended up with the RD–180 engine?

General SHELTON. The Evolved Expendable Launch Vehicle (EELV) program was originally developed as a commercial program and foreign-sourced engines were permitted. In addition, the use of foreign components or technologies in upgrading U.S. space transportation was encouraged through the Space Modernization Plan as part of the Moorman Study (1994). In 1995, the Secretary of Defense established policy (e.g. stockpiling) to ensure U.S. access to space is not jeopardized by delays or disruptions of former Soviet Union-produced systems, components, or technology. The Russian-made RD–180 engine was proposed by Lockheed Martin for Atlas V as part of the 1998 EELV competition because it offered significant cost, schedule, and performance benefits. The use of the RD–180 was approved by the Department of Defense (DOD).

The original 1998 plan was to co-produce the RD–180 in the United States to comply with policy regarding use of former Soviet Union produced propulsion systems. The policy was changed in 2000 in order to reduce the risk of foreign dependence and allowed for buying RD–180s ahead of need and storing. In 2007, DOD deferred and eventually eliminated the requirement to co-produce the RD–180 in the United States due in part to the expected expense ($1 billion+) of co-production. United Launch Alliance (ULA) maintains a stockpile of RD–180 engines to mitigate the risk of supply interruption. Another reason why the co-production requirement was eliminated was the availability of the Delta IV family, powered by U.S. developed and produced engines. The Air Force regularly reviews and analyzes various components of the EELV program to include any potential risks associated with the use of RD–180 engines.

2. Senator UDALL. General Shelton, it is my understanding that the U.S. Government encouraged the use of former Soviet Union capabilities in prior administrations and that encouragement led to the use of the RD–180 engine on one of two certified EELV systems. Is this your understanding of the history?

General SHELTON. Yes, the EELV program was originally developed as a commercial program and foreign-sourced engines were permitted. In addition, the use of foreign components or technologies in upgrading U.S. space transportation was encouraged through the Space Modernization Plan as part of the Moorman Study (1994). In 1995, the Secretary of Defense established policy (e.g. stockpiling) to ensure U.S. access to space is not jeopardized by delays or disruptions of former Soviet Union-produced systems, components, or technology. The Russian-made RD–180 engine was proposed by Lockheed Martin for Atlas V as part of the 1998 EELV competition because it offered significant cost, schedule, and performance benefits. The use of the RD–180 was approved by DOD.

The original 1998 plan was to co-produce the RD–180 in the U.S. to comply with policy regarding use of former Soviet Union produced propulsion systems. The policy was changed in 2000 in order to reduce the risk of foreign dependence and allowed for buying RD–180s ahead of need and storing. In 2007, DOD deferred and eventually eliminated the requirement to co-produce the RD–180 in the United States due in part to the expected expense ($1 billion+) of co-production. ULA maintains a stockpile of RD–180 engines to mitigate the risk of supply interruption. Another reason why the co-production requirement was eliminated was the availability of the Delta IV family, powered by U.S. developed and produced engines. The Air Force regularly reviews and analyzes various components of the EELV program to include any potential risks associated with the use of RD–180 engines.

3. Senator UDALL. General Shelton, have the engines and all the support provided the foreign and domestic contractors met all U.S. Government requirements for this program?

General SHELTON. Yes, the RD–180, RS–68, and RL–10 engines and their suppliers meet the U.S. Government's requirements.

4. Senator UDALL. General Shelton, did ULA, the EELV incumbent contractor, obtain the blueprints and specifications of the RD–180 engine?

General SHELTON. Yes, ULA, acting through Aerojet Rocketdyne (previously Pratt-Whitney) and RD Amross, has all the information to produce RD–180 engines in the United States and is in discussions with NPO Energomash to increase the license period from 2022 through 2030.

5. Senator UDALL. General Shelton, with the Air Force technical oversight by DOD and Federally Funded Research and Development Centers, did contractor personnel go through a process of demonstrating the ability to build some of the most complex components and conduct independent design analysis to demonstrate the ability to produce the engine in country, if required?

General SHELTON. Yes. During the early acquisition activities of the EELV program, a three-phase co-production effort was initiated to develop a domestic production capability for the RD–180 engine. In the first two phases of this effort, executed from 1996 through 1998, the engine vendor (Pratt-Whitney Rocketdyne at the time) completed an initial design assessment and demonstrated 12 key manufacturing processes. These activities also included the production of several key components. The third phase of the effort was intended to fully demonstrate the capability of implementing domestic co-production and ran from the early 2000s through mid-2008, when the effort was deferred. During this phase, 10 of the original 12 manufacturing processes were re-demonstrated and some of the more complex components were produced and tested. This included manufacturing and burst testing of a domestically-produced full-scale preburner and stator. Throughout the co-production effort, an independent design analysis was also completed for significant portion of the engine components.

ACQUISITION STRATEGY

6. Senator UDALL. General Shelton, would you please comment on the report that an independent team of DOD experts conducted a study to determine the earliest possible time a new entrant would be close to being certified and capable to launch any or all of the EELV missions?

General SHELTON. The independent team assessed probable certification dates, analyzing the schedule using common statistical (Monte Carlo) analysis. The team concluded the new entrant would most likely be certified by the second quarter of fiscal year 2015 (80 percent probability), but that the earliest they would be certified was probably best represented by the company's own schedule. As a note, in deciding when to compete, we used the company's own schedule.

7. Senator UDALL. General Shelton, would you please comment on the readiness of any new entrant to compete, when will they be certified, and will they have all the capabilities to launch all National Security Space (NSS) payloads?

General SHELTON. New entrants are required to be certified for contract award, but are allowed to compete once telemetry data from the final certification flight have been submitted. The Air Force and SpaceX are working aggressively toward certification of the Falcon 9 v1.1 by December 2014. However, certification is an event-driven, not schedule-driven, process which requires all activities and assessments to be complete and the launch system deemed low risk.

SpaceX is not seeking certification for all eight of the DOD reference orbits at this time. Due to weight limitations to the Falcon 9 v1.1 and the orbits for which SpaceX is seeking certification, the Falcon 9 v1.1 rocket will not have the capability to launch all NSS payloads.

8. Senator UDALL. General Shelton, why did the missions available for competition decrease from the planned up-to-14, to up-to-7?

General SHELTON. The Air Force re-phased five Global Positioning System (GPS) III satellites (GPS III 7/8/9/10/11) due to our revised forecasted operational need. Of the eight GPS III missions originally identified for potential competition in 2015 to 2017, five have been delayed to 2018 to 2023. They remain available for competition, albeit a later time. These GPS changes were the result of careful sustainment of our on-orbit satellites, allowing us to project additional satellite lifetime without increased risk to the satellite constellations. This results in almost $400 million less required for space launch over the Future Years Defense Program (FYDP).

The AFSPC–8 mission was reallocated due to mission requirements. Additionally, per the Cooperative Research and Development Agreement signed between SpaceX and the Air Force, SpaceX is not pursuing certification to this orbit.

Finally, SBIRS GEO–4 was provisionally moved to the Phase 1 Block Buy to maintain the 36 core commitment.

The Air Force continually reassesses constellation health for all its on-orbit assets and updates programming accordingly. Through subsequent POM cycles, AFSPC will annually reassess and adjust planned procurements as operational requirements, Space Vehicle development/production, and fiscal realities dictate.

It is important to note that, under the Phase 1 Block Buy, the Air Force orders launch vehicle configurations that can support multiple missions to enable mission assignment as late as 12 months prior to launch.

9. Senator UDALL. General Shelton, is it fair to say that the second phase, the so-called phase 1A of the Air Force acquisition strategy, that both the new entrant and the incumbent launch provider were equally hurt in the decision to reduce the number of missions for competition?

General SHELTON. The Air Force cannot speculate about the impact of reduced competitions on industry. The decision to reduce the number of missions available for Phase 1A competition was due to satellite constellation requirements changes. These changes were the result of careful sustainment of our on-orbit satellites, allowing us to assume additional satellite lifetime without increased risk to the satellite constellations. The Air Force has taken advantage of the extraordinary efforts by the operators at Air Force Space Command to delay launch procurements, resulting in almost $400 million less required for space launch over the FYDP.

It is important to note that all missions designated for competitive missions are available for all launch service providers, including certified new entrants and incumbents. The Air Force is committed to competition within the EELV program, and we are currently evaluating options to move additional competitive opportunities into Phase IA.

10. Senator UDALL. General Shelton, what would it take to increase the competitive missions back to up-to-14?

General SHELTON. Along with an operational need, new funding to procure the additional launch services and adjustments to budget to accelerate delivery of new production satellites would be required to increase the number of competitive missions.

11. Senator UDALL. General Shelton, does the Air Force currently have a need for those satellite launches?

General SHELTON. No, the Air Force's current operational launch needs are reflected in the fiscal year 2015 President's budget request.

–––––––

QUESTION SUBMITTED BY SENATOR ANGUS S. KING, JR.

EXPLANATION OF CONFIGURATION TYPES

21. Senator KING. General Shelton, during the hearing you mentioned that the SpaceX Falcon 9 will likely only be able to support 3 of the 10 configuration types that the Atlas V currently supports. Would you please explain what these three configuration types entail and give more details regarding what key steps remain for

certification of SpaceX so that it can compete for the seven open competition missions?

General SHELTON. The Atlas V has multiple configurations; the configuration is indicated by a three digit number. The first digit indicates the diameter of the payload faring, which is the part enclosing the payload and protecting it during launch. On an Atlas V, this is either 4 meters or 5 meters. The second digit indicates the number of solid boosters, ranging from 0 to 5. The third digit indicates the number of RL–10 engines, 1 or 2.

The Falcon 9v1.1 is most comparable in terms of capability to four configurations of the Atlas V (401, 411, 501, and 511). Each of these configurations has one RL–10 engine and either zero or one solid booster.

There are three phases in the certification process (assessment, evaluation, and certification). SpaceX is currently in the middle of the evaluation phase. New entrants are required to be certified for contract award, but are allowed to compete once telemetry data from the final certification flight have been submitted. The Air Force and SpaceX are working aggressively toward certification by December 2014.

———

QUESTIONS SUBMITTED BY SENATOR BILL NELSON

SOLID ROCKET MOTORS

12. Senator NELSON. Ms. Chaplain, you mentioned in your testimony the strategic need for maintaining solid rocket motors. How do you suggest that the need for solid rocket motors be factored into the government–wide approach that you are proposing?

Ms. CHAPLAIN. Solid rocket motors are an important part DOD weapons programs. They are used as supplementary boosters to the launch vehicles in the EELV program, and may be used in the National Aeronautics and Space Administration (NASA) new Space Launch System (SLS). In addition, the industrial base for these motors supports not only the EELV and NASA programs but also is shared with other important weapons programs such as strategic missiles. Since solid rocket motors will likely be a part of an architecture that replaces the Atlas 5 launch vehicle, decisions could have an impact on other programs that depend on solid rocket motors and on the industrial base. Thus, they should be made in a government-wide context, that is, DOD should seek input from NASA and industry about the impacts associated with decisions on technologies, designs, and planned use. Moreover, DOD has found that it needs to better define its long-term needs for solid rocket motors and that it must preserve the scientific, engineering, and design skills and production capacity of the industry.

SPACE LAUNCH SYSTEM

13. Senator NELSON. Mr. Lightfoot, could the NASA SLS variants eventually provide another domestic option for launching national security payloads or other NASA missions?

Mr. LIGHTFOOT. SLS is designed for the purpose of enabling human exploration beyond low-Earth orbit in support of national objectives and policy. In addition, consistent with existing law and policy, SLS is not to compete with commercial space transportation services provided by U.S. commercial companies, but is potentially available to support national priorities that may require SLS-unique capabilities, and/or provide an avenue for U.S. access to space should reliable U.S. commercial capabilities not be available.

NEW ENGINE DEVELOPMENT PROGRAMS

14. Senator NELSON. Ms. Chaplain and Mr. Dumbacher, both NASA and DOD have previously invested in engine development programs. However, some of these programs have been cancelled or have experienced significant cost growth. What best practices should be implemented to ensure the success of a new development program?

Ms. CHAPLAIN. Our past work on acquisition best practices has highlighted the need for agencies—including DOD and NASA, to first match system requirements with available resources—the knowledge, time, and money necessary to meet those requirements, before committing a project—and necessary money—to development. Technology readiness level assessments and systems engineering reviews are critical metrics for agencies to use in order to assess whether or not resources available will meet the program's requirements. Moreover, our best practices work has shown that successful new programs sought to utilize the most mature technology available instead of attempting to design a program that required significant amounts of new technical content. It is also critical that once requirements have been set and subsequently matched to available resources, those requirements should be held stable. Our work has shown that this is best done by conducting early systems engineering analysis of requirements, working closely with industry to ensure requirements are clearly defined and then making trade-offs as necessary. In addition, programs need to avoid schedule-driven development, and allow adequate time for a disciplined technology development processes. Many problems in DOD weapons system development programs have been tied to programs attempting to meet unrealistic schedules. Our best practices work has also shown the importance of considering the cost to operate and maintain systems prior to committing a program to development.

Our reviews of some of the canceled rocket development programs you refer to also point out some important lessons learned. For instance, in 2001, we reported that NASA did not prepare risk management plans for its ambitious X–33 and X–34 programs until several years after the projects were implemented nor mechanisms for ensuring the completion of the program if significant cost growth occurred and/or the business case motivating industry participation weakened substantially. Moreover, communications within the program and with contractors about potential problems such as those with the composite fuel tank were not effective. The lessons from these programs are important because they represented an effort to establish a partnership with industry. On a subsequent canceled program, Constellation, we reported that a poorly phased funding plan contributed to delays and limited NASA's ability to mitigate technical risks early in development and precluded the orderly ramp up of workforce and development activities.

Mr. DUMBACHER. First and foremost, to ensure success of a development program, the top level design requirements or needs must be clearly understood and defined by all stakeholders. Prior to starting such a development program, sufficient resources to meet the requirements should be identified based upon the management structure, scope necessary to meet the requirements, and required schedule. It is essential that sufficient schedule and budget margins be established and protected throughout the entire program lifecycle to address technical and programmatic issues as they arise.

REDUCING LAUNCH COSTS

15. Senator NELSON. Ms. Chaplain, based on your previous experience, what opportunities are there to reduce total long-term launch costs?

Ms. CHAPLAIN. The Air Force has taken some significant steps towards reducing long-term launch costs, including conducting in-depth reviews of the program's cost drivers and using the data it collected through these reviews to negotiate lower launch prices with ULA. In addition, our past work has shown that competition can help to lower prices, and the potential for new entrants to the EELV-class launch market also likely helped to lower launch prices. One area that should be explored further is potential duplication and overlap between NASA and DOD launch acquisition activities and launch infrastructure. GAO has examined this question to a limited extent. The agencies themselves can do this if they apply a government-wide perspective to their own program planning and work with other agencies to make sure investments are not duplicative or suboptimal. A second area is having a complete picture of government-wide launch costs and planned investments. This information could help to inform plans to lower launch costs, increase competition, and invest in new programs but it has been lacking. GAO's 2013 review of government-wide launch costs could be used as a starting point for such assessments.

WHOLE-OF-GOVERNMENT APPROACH

16. Senator NELSON. Ms. Chaplain, what opportunities are specifically tied to taking a whole-of-government approach?

Ms. CHAPLAIN. By having a more coordinated, government-wide launch strategy or policy, the government might be able to better leverage its buying power towards getting the best possible procurement deal with each launch services provider. In addition, a whole-of-government approach to launch services acquisitions may allow the government to reduce duplication in the current acquisition process. For example, in the current process, DOD and NASA contract separately for launch services from each launch provider, using different processes to certify launch vehicles and different contract mechanisms and workforces to manage the contracts. A detailed assessment of these areas could identify opportunities to consolidate work and simplify processes, without increasing launch risk. In addition, by having a coordinated plan or policy, the government could look at the launch enterprise as one entity benefiting the entire government, optimize investments and funding in the most efficient and effective way possible, and target these investments towards benefitting all government groups that use launch services. We acknowledge that there are substantial challenges to this approach, particularly the different launch services acquisition approaches among government launch customers, as well as somewhat different auxiliary launch needs, such as mission assurance and security. However, if the benefit to a coordinated approach, such as simplified and less duplicative processes, would likely outweigh the challenges and risks to adopting such an approach.

———

QUESTIONS SUBMITTED BY SENATOR TIM KAINE

SMALL AND MEDIUM NATIONAL SECURITY SPACE PAYLOADS

17. Senator KAINE. General Shelton and Mr. Lightfoot, Wallops Island Flight Facility provides critical services to medium-sized space launches for both commercial and NSS purposes. Some NSS payloads that are part of the EELV construct can be launched from facilities like Wallops on smaller launch vehicles, which is more cost-effective than larger launchers. For example, the Defense Meteorological Satellite Program (DMSP) is a small-to-medium class satellite that can be delivered by Minotaur VI, Delta II, and Antares. The latter, Antares, was developed by Orbital Sciences Corporation and is slated to carry eight cargo missions out of Wallops to the International Space Station (ISS) through 2016. In your view, what are the benefits of using small- and mid-sized launches and launch capabilities to launch smaller NSS missions like DMSP, rather than larger rockets?

General SHELTON. When combined with the ability to launch multiple payloads on a single vehicle, the Air Force is able to better procure launch services and pursue certain missions that would have previously been cost prohibitive. Using small- and mid-sized launches and launch capabilities to launch smaller NSS missions allows us to maximize the cost and schedule efficiency of our launch services procurement. Launching smaller NSS missions can potentially reduce costs, but only in the case where the associated excess capacity of the larger rocket is not being used to carry additional payloads.

The current DMSP Block 5D–3 satellite weighs 2,720 pounds at liftoff (with booster adapter). The Block 5D–3 has been launched on the following launch vehicles: Atlas V, Delta IV, and Titan II. Integration on any vehicle would add a year to launch schedule imposing extra storage and integration costs.

Conceivably, DMSP can be launched on any launch vehicle capable of putting 2,500 pounds into a polar orbit from the West Coast. That said, no studies have been conducted to indicate if DMSP could go on Minotaur, Delta II, or Antares, or even Falcon 9, for that matter. To answer the question we would have to study the loads and possibly make software changes to DMSP to assess the feasibility of using small launch vehicles.

Weather system follow-on programs, with smaller satellites, could potentially benefit from the availability of multiple launch options at a lower cost using smaller launch vehicles. Additional launch options introduce competition and drive down costs, while improving manifest scheduling flexibility. The ability to launch smaller satellites on smaller launch vehicles will make space more commercially viable.

Mr. LIGHTFOOT. The physical size and weight of the satellite, along with the lift energy required to reach the intended orbit or destination in space, determines the necessary size of a rocket that launches from a given launch point. From a NASA perspective, the benefits of using small- and medium-sized launchers to launch small- and medium-sized primary payloads are that these launchers are typically much less expensive than the large EELV-class rockets, thereby reducing overall mission costs for small- and medium-class missions. In addition, small- and medium-class launchers provide a dedicated ride for small- and medium-class missions that place the satellite directly into its proper orbit, and are able to fly when the satellite is ready to launch.

18. Senator KAINE. General Shelton and Mr. Lightfoot, as space technology advances, do you see a trend in the direction of smaller NSS payloads with increased capability replacing larger payloads?

General SHELTON. Yes, I see a trend toward smaller NSS payloads. This is enabled by improved technology (smaller payloads with the same or better performance as previous systems) and more efficient and flexible launch options. Continued study into future smaller NSS payloads is ongoing in an effort to enhance resiliency in current space architecture through disaggregation. Although smaller payloads may not be appropriate in all mission areas, potential opportunities to meeting mission requirements with smaller NSS payloads are being investigated.

Mr. LIGHTFOOT. NASA defers to DOD for the assessment of trends related to NSS payloads.

REPLACING U.S. DEPENDENCY ON THE RUSSIAN RD–180

19. Senator KAINE. Mr. Estevez, the United States, between the government and private sector, has already invested nearly $300 million in risk reduction activities related to advanced oxygen rich staged combustion technology that will equal or exceed the performance of the RD–180. On the government side, these efforts have included the Air Force's Hydrocarbon Booster Technology Program and the NASA's Advanced Booster Engineering Demonstration and Risk Reduction Program. Both of these currently active contracts were competitively awarded in 2007 and 2013, respectively. The U.S. rocket engine industrial base has experience in purchasing, disassembling, modifying, and launching Russian engines of the same basic type as the RD–180. It also has the advantage of utilizing modern technologies such as additive manufacturing and improved metallurgy. Based upon these facts and the experience gained executing ongoing risk reduction activities, industry experts estimate that with proper funding they can develop an advanced liquid rocket engine in 4 years. Would you please explain how you determined the time required to develop an alternative engine?

Mr. ESTEVEZ. Initial government estimates for the cost and time required to develop an alternative engine are based, in part, from review of the Aerojet-Rocketdyne RS–68 development program. This engine is the main propulsion system for the Delta IV first stage and, though using a different fuel, is the most recent comparable experience in class and capability. This initial estimate was at least $2.9 billion and 8 years. More refined cost and schedule estimates will be prepared as DOD moves forward with its evaluation of future domestic propulsion and launch vehicle capabilities.

20. Senator KAINE. Mr. Estevez, do you believe it is necessary that we restart already completed risk reduction work?

Mr. ESTEVEZ. DOD has an ongoing rocket motor technology risk reduction program that currently has a completion date targeted for fiscal year 2021. The fiscal year 2014 omnibus reprograming action had $40 million included to accelerate the program focusing on several high return-on-investment activities, such as combustion modeling and full-scale component testing. This program is leveraging previous risk reduction activity and building on those findings, not restarting or repeating them.

QUESTIONS SUBMITTED BY SENATOR JEFF SESSIONS

RD–180 REPLACEMENT FUNDING

22. Senator SESSIONS. General Shelton, late last week DOD sent Congress a reprograming request that included a request for $40 million to begin "Technology Risk Reduction for Commercial New Engine Development." According to the explanation for the request, the funds are needed to develop strategies and initiate engine risk reduction efforts, technology maturation activities, and early concept studies and surveys. It goes on to state that the funding will focus on "key risk components, technology development work on engine components of diverse types, requirements definitions, and maturation of key components." I am fully supportive of the funding request; however, I am concerned that the explanation is signaling a piecemeal approach that will never result in an engine replacement and keeps us reliant on Russia. You know the history of this program better than anyone; do you agree with my concern that if we fail to act now, we are very likely to fall back into the same complacency that got us in this mess in the first place?

General SHELTON. I agree with your concern that this is an appropriate time to commit to and pursue a next generation domestic engine program, both to assure reliable space access well into the future and reduce our reliance on foreign-made engines. The reprogramming request for $40 million is an immediate effort to reduce technical risk prior to a full-scale propulsion system development, by focusing on key systems and technologies. The work described in the reprogramming request is a necessary precursor to full-scale development, and should position the Air Force to hit the ground running on that effort. The particulars of the full-scale engine development effort are still in work, and will be delivered in a plan from the Secretary of the Air Force in coordination with the NASA Administrator.

23. Senator SESSIONS. General Shelton, in your personal opinion, do you believe we should be more aggressive than the piecemeal approach that is being signaled in the reprograming request?

General SHELTON. No. In my personal opinion, the effort described in the reprogramming request is, in fact, aggressive, and should position the Air Force well for a full-scale propulsion system development. That full effort assumes additional funding in fiscal year 2015 and/or fiscal year 2016. Full scale development contract(s) will begin as soon as the technology maturation is complete.

24. Senator SESSIONS. General Shelton, why didn't the reprograming request identify a date to complete this engine by?

General SHELTON. We are in the process of reaching out to industry and requesting their inputs to better inform our decisionmaking regarding potential options. Additionally, we are discussing the matter with key government stakeholders. As a preferred course of action becomes evident, we will identify required completion dates. Our current estimate is that a new engine would require 5 to 8 years to complete, but we are continuing to refine that estimate as we obtain better information.

25. Senator SESSIONS. General Shelton, the reprograming request states that there are no funds in the fiscal year 2015 budget for this effort. You are certainly aware that each of the congressional defense committees that have reported their bills out of committee thus far has included at least $100 million for the new engine in fiscal year 2015. Do you agree that if we are to replace the RD–180 by 2019 or shortly thereafter, funding will be required in fiscal year 2015 and across the FYDP?

General SHELTON. Yes, funding will be required in fiscal year 2015 and across the FYDP. The reprogramming request was completed based on the fiscal year 2015 President's budget, which did not contain any funds for a new engine development effort.

ADDITIONAL EELV LAUNCH IN FISCAL YEAR 2015

26. Senator SESSIONS. Mr. Estevez and General Shelton, the omnibus reprograming request included a request for a $100 million increase to fund an additional fiscal year 2015 launch that can be competitively awarded while maintaining the 36 core block buy. According to the justification materials, the funds are anticipated to be used to add DMSP #20 to the manifest. I appreciate that DOD appears to be following this committee's reported bill guidance on adding an additional competitive opportunity in fiscal year 2015. However, I am concerned with the decision to use DMSP #20 as that additional launch. Just a few months ago with the budget release, we were told that the reason the Air Force terminated the launch for DMSP #20 in the first place was because of the high cost of long-term storage and the low added mission benefit of launching DMSP #20. It is my understanding that there are no hard Air Force or DOD requirements which are satisfied by launching DMSP #20. What has changed requirements-wise since that decision not to launch DMSP #20 was made?

Mr. ESTEVEZ. DOD's requirements have not changed. Although DMSP–20 has capabilities that support many of DOD's space-based environmental monitoring (SBEM) requirements, the recently completed and JROC approved SBEM Analysis of Alternatives (AoA) determined that these requirements could be met by civil and international partner systems with acceptable risks. The fiscal year 2014 omnibus reprogramming request did include funding for an additional competitively awarded launch in fiscal year 2015, and DMSP–20 was identified as an option, but the manifest for the additional launch was not set. The fiscal year 2015 appropriations bill language has directed launch of DMSP–20 by the end of calendar year 2016. DOD is currently evaluating its ability to comply with this direction.

General SHELTON. Nothing has changed. While DMSP–20 has capabilities supporting multiple Air Force and DOD space-based environmental monitoring requirements, the recently completed SBEM AoA determined these requirements could be allocated with acceptable risk to civil and international partner systems.

The final decision on which mission the launch service will procure will be made based on multiple factors, including launch manifest requirements and available competitive opportunities for new entrants.

27. Senator SESSIONS. Mr. Estevez and General Shelton, is it true that the launch of DMSP #20 is being pushed by the White House on behalf of the National Oceanic and Atmospheric Administration?

Mr. ESTEVEZ. I am not aware of a request from the National Oceanic and Atmospheric Administration to DOD to launch DMSP #20. The President's budget request for fiscal year 2015 enables DOD to continue service-life extension, integration, and test activities for DMSP #20 during fiscal year 2015. Continuing these activities enables DOD to prepare to launch and operate DMSP #20 successfully, if and when the decision is made to do so. Based on the finding from the SBEM AoA, DOD is currently working with the Executive Office of the President to review the benefit of launching DMSP #20.

General SHELTON. I do not know if that is the case. What I do know is that the fiscal year 2015 President's budget request for DMSP enables DOD to continue post-Service Life Extension Program Integration and Test of DMSP F–20 in fiscal year 2015 and avoid taking irreversible actions that would preclude the satellite from being launched and operated successfully on-orbit.

28. Senator SESSIONS. Mr. Estevez and General Shelton, what was the justification for terminating the launch for DMSP #20 when DOD submitted the fiscal year 2015 budget earlier this year?

Mr. ESTEVEZ. DOD considered terminating the launch of DMSP #20 because the SBEM AoA suggested that contributions from civil and international partner systems could satisfy some of the Department's weather gaps. However, the decision was made to continue preparing DMSP #20 for launch during fiscal year 2015. Based on the finding from the SBEM AoA, DOD is currently working with Executive Office of the President to review the benefit of launching DMSP #20.

General SHELTON. The justification for proposing to terminate the DMSP F–20 launch was based on the SBEM AoA findings which identified that civil and international contributions are adequately supporting several of the key requirements. The Air Force plans to focus its resources to develop the future Weather System Follow-on (WSF) program which will fulfill the gaps that won't be sufficiently covered by DMSP, civil, or international systems.

29. Senator SESSIONS. General Shelton, is it your professional military opinion that spending almost $200 million to launch DMSP #20, $100 million identified for the launch and the accompanying $80 million to store the satellite—which this committee already cut from the budget—is the best place to allocate our resources given our current fiscal concerns?

General SHELTON. The direct answer is no, I don't believe this is the best use of resources. While I understand the desire for another competitive launch, I believe the best use of resources for the environmental monitoring mission is to focus on the unique DOD requirements identified in the SBEM AoA. By pursuing the WSF program instead of launching DMSP #20 (which doesn't fully satisfy those requirements), we can avoid continued funding of a dedicated DMSP payload processing facility at Vandenberg, we can avoid paying the storage costs for DMSP #20, and we would not have to fund a booster for that satellite (the WSF would likely be launched by a small booster). An additional consideration is the cost of integrating DMSP #20 onto any booster other than Atlas V or Delta IV (it is already dual-integrated on those).

IMPACT OF SPACEX LITIGATION ON DEFENSE ACQUISITION

30. Senator SESSIONS. Mr. Estevez, according to a recent Department of Justice motion to dismiss the litigation brought by SpaceX in the Court of Federal Claims, the U.S. Government claims that SpaceX lacks standing to bring a challenge because SpaceX was not a qualified bidder at the time the Air Force issued its Request for Proposal (RFP). According to the U.S. Government's motion to dismiss, SpaceX is not an interested party to the block buy contract because while SpaceX knew about the intent of the Air Force to award that contract and received a copy of the solicitation, for SpaceX to be an interested party, they should have filed a statement of interest or lodged a complaint long before the contract was awarded. Essentially, SpaceX waived its right to challenge the block buy by not challenging the contract during the RFP period, prior to the contracts award. Given your position as the Principal Deputy Under Secretary of Defense for Acquisition, Technology, and Logistics, if the court does not grant the motion to dismiss, what could this mean for other defense acquisitions?

Mr. ESTEVEZ. Since DOD is presently engaged in litigation before the U.S. Court of Federal Claims on the EELV program, we cannot comment on the motions filed before the Court. When the Court issues its decision, DOD will review its impact on the EELV and other defense acquisition programs.

BLOCK BUY AND COMPETITION

31. Senator SESSIONS. Mr. Estevez and General Shelton, new entrants have stated that they feel the Air Force has been slow in its approval process and that they believe their rocket is ready to launch NSS payloads right now. Did the Commercial Research and Development Agreement (CRADA) that SpaceX entered into prior to beginning the certification process lay out everything that was expected of them and timelines for certification?

Mr. ESTEVEZ. The CRADA that SpaceX entered into with the Air Force Space and Missile Systems Center includes an attachment titled Falcon 9 v1.1 Certification Plan. The certification plan details the requirements including the timeline for the certification approach individually selected, and agreed to, by Space X. The certification timeline is based on the successful completion of a specified number of launches and technical reviews. The length of time to complete the technical reviews is dependent upon the quality of the data submissions.

General SHELTON. Yes, the CRADA signed by the Air Force and SpaceX June 7, 2013, laid out everything that was expected of SpaceX to achieve certification. The CRADA does not spell out certification timelines as completion of certification is an event-driven process requiring completion of exit criteria as defined within the CRADA.

32. Senator SESSIONS. Mr. Estevez and General Shelton, isn't it true that SpaceX could have avoided the long study of technical data by launching more, so was it their choice to pursue the current certification process?

Mr. ESTEVEZ. SpaceX chose their certification path from the multiple options provided in the New Entrant Certification Guide (NECG). As an example, the NECG Category 3 (low risk) certification approach requires anywhere from 14 launches with very little data delivery requirements to 2 launches with significant data delivery and review requirements.

General SHELTON. Yes, the U.S. Air Force launch services NECG outlines four possible alternatives to achieve the Category 3 (low risk) certification required by the EELV program. These alternatives require as many as 14 flights, and as few as 2 flights, with fewer flights requiring increased technical evaluation for certification.

33. Senator SESSIONS. Mr. Estevez and General Shelton, why is the certification process necessary?

Mr. ESTEVEZ. The certification process is necessary because DOD does not purchase launch insurance, as commercial launch service customers do, and the certification process is the first step in our integrated mission assurance process that maximizes the probability of successfully launching and deploying critical NSS payloads. As the U.S. Government was not involved in the new entrant's launch vehicle design process, it is incumbent on us to verify that all new entrants meet the EELV program requirements for a launch vehicle design reliability of 98 percent and an overall system level reliability of 97 percent. The certification process allows DOD to have sufficient insight into a launch system so that it may act as an informed consumer when purchasing launch services to launch operational national security spacecraft. Additionally, certification provides the foundation for the flight-worthiness certification process, part of the recurring mission assurance activities for every NSS mission.

The impact of a launch failure can be significant in both dollars and loss of critical capabilities. A single NSS operational payload can cost from hundreds of millions of dollars upward to over a billion dollars and may be designed to provide unique capabilities not available from other systems. Because of these potential significant impacts from the loss of a single payload, it is critical that DOD understand the reliability of all systems utilized to launch critical NSS payloads.

General SHELTON. The certification process is necessary to protect valuable government assets and ensure continued satisfaction of NSS mission requirements. NSS missions typically involve highly sensitive and very expensive payloads. Between 1997 and 1999, our country experienced a string of launch failures of which the value of those payloads lost exceeded $3 billion. Also lost were national security and warfighter capabilities those payloads were expected to provide.

Additionally, certification actually allows us to reduce the risk of new entrants and facilitates their ability to compete in a best-value environment that considers mission risk. Without the certification process, a new entrant would likely be less competitive given the lack of a mission success track record and the importance of mission risk in consideration of best value.

34. Senator SESSIONS. Mr. Estevez and General Shelton, what are you hoping to learn from the certification process?

Mr. ESTEVEZ. DOD expects to develop insight into the new entrant's launch system design and process reliability, which is a critical component in the overall EELV program's mission assurance process. Understanding of the new entrant's vehicle design and reliability, developed through the system's certification process, will be used to help tailor the recurring mission assurance activities that occur on each and every NSS launch operation. The insight into the vehicle design developed during the certification process allows DOD to focus the recurring missions assurance activities, minimizing cost to both the contractor and the government, while maximizing the probability of a successful launch.

General SHELTON. The purpose of the certification process is to ensure successful launches by determining if new entrants are capable of meeting Air Force established launch requirements. The Air Force has established standards that all launch providers must meet. Formal design and mission reliability assessments are necessary to ensure the launch system capability to provide the necessary payload mass-to-orbit, orbital insertion accuracy, and other requirements to place a healthy payload into its intended orbit for maximum utility. We expect the certification process to produce new entrants that are ready to compete for NSS missions by resolving any launch anomalies and demonstrating a track record of mission success.

35. Senator SESSIONS. Mr. Estevez and General Shelton, have any SpaceX launches had any issues that could be a concern?

Mr. ESTEVEZ. SpaceX has launched its three certification flights for the Falcon 9 v1.1. The flights occurred on September 29, 2013; December 3, 2013; and January 6, 2014, and all inserted their payloads into their intended orbits and therefore have been declared successful by the Air Force Space and Missile Systems Center Commander. Even though categorized as successes during each mission, anomalies requiring post flight analysis occurred, which is not uncommon to space launch operations. All flight data associated with SpaceX launches is considered company proprietary and thus I am unable to discuss any anomalies in my response. DOD continues to evaluate available data from the certification missions to ensure it understands the details of the anomalies and their possible impact on future launch operations.

General SHELTON. Yes, SpaceX has had issues on each of their certification flights. SpaceX is working within their anomaly resolution process to resolve these issues and, per the CRADA, working with the Air Force to address any certification impacts.

36. Senator SESSIONS. Mr. Estevez and General Shelton, this certification process is new for everyone; what do you believe the Air Force can do better to help streamline its process in the future to either shorten the time to certify or to better educate new entrants on the requirements?

Mr. ESTEVEZ. The certification process was developed to ensure that all new entrants meet the EELV program launch system design and process reliability standards. The process is designed to provide the U.S. Government an in-depth understanding of the new entrants's system. In order to minimize the impact on the prospective suppliers, the NECG was developed with multiple certification levels and approaches, thus allowing the new entrants to select the certification approach most compatible with existing company processes and practices. While the NECG clearly delineates the certification requirements, in the future, spending some additional time informing a prospective new entrants to the intent and scope of the requirements prior to the beginning of the certification process is a lesson learned that we will apply to future new entrants certifications.

General SHELTON. The NECG, published in 2011 and based on proven NASA certification processes, provides a risk-based approach with multiple options to achieving certification to allow for flexibility with different timelines based on maturity of the launch system. However, certification is an event-driven, not schedule-driven, process. All requirements for certification are agreed to in any CRADA that would be signed by a new entrant seeking certification.

The multiple alternatives available are based on an Air Force, NRO, and NASA developed joint strategy document titled, "Coordinated Strategy Among the United

States Air Force; The National Reconnaissance Office; and The National Aeronautics and Space Administration on New Entrant Launch Vehicle Certification," signed on October 12, 2011. In the strategy, the launch organizations agreed to adopt a certification framework consistent with NASA Policy Directive (NPD) 8610.7. This framework provides a methodology for certification of launch vehicles based on risk classifications for individual payloads.

RECERTIFICATION OF THE ATLAS V

37. Senator SESSIONS. Mr. Estevez and General Shelton, once a domestic engine is developed to replace the RD–180, I suspect the Atlas V launch vehicle will have to be recertified with the new engine. Has DOD identified what that recertification process may look like?

Mr. ESTEVEZ. In the event of a significant configuration change requiring recertification, any launch service provider will be expected to follow the guidance in the NECG. There are multiple paths to certification and we leave it to the provider's judgment to select their preferred approach.

General SHELTON. It would be premature to project what the final solution will be to address the concern about reliance to foreign engines; however, if an Air Force mission involves a significant change to the vehicle configuration or employs a previously undemonstrated mission profile, the launch provider must present design and qualification data for review and approval by the Air Force Space and Missile Center as part of the flight worthiness certification process.

WAIVERS FOR SPACEX CERTIFICATION

38. Senator SESSIONS. Mr. Estevez and General Shelton, did the Air Force give SpaceX any waivers regarding the need to meet all orbital regimes or provide additional time for SpaceX to achieve certain critical capabilities such as vertical integration of satellites?

Mr. ESTEVEZ. When the SpaceX entered into the CRADA with the Air Force in June 2013, it was with the understanding that certification would be issued with limitations in the following areas: (1) verification of only four of the eight required reference orbits; (2) implementation of a secure flight termination system; (3) implementation of a GPS metric tracking system; (4) demonstration of a vertical integration capability; and (5) obtaining an ISO 2700 information assurance certification. Areas 2 through 5 will have to be implemented prior to the launch of any NSS mission. If SpaceX decides to compete for missions in addition to the 4 specified in the CRADA, additional verification will be required. Space X is currently seeking certification for the following reference orbits: (1) 500 nautical mile circular Low Earth Orbit; (2) 450 nautical mile Sun Synchronous; (3) 55 degree inclination Semi-Synchronous Orbit; and (4) GEO transfer Orbit (GTO).

General SHELTON. SpaceX has been given no waivers to EELV program requirements. The CRADA covers EELV certification for SpaceX, which is a necessary precondition for launching NSS missions. The requirements for each launch service are specific to that mission, and SpaceX can only compete for those missions for which they are seeking certification, currently four of the eight DOD reference orbits. Vertical integration is a necessary precondition for launching NSS missions and must be demonstrated and verified 12 months prior to launch.

39. Senator SESSIONS. Mr. Estevez and General Shelton, does the Air Force have any concerns with the SpaceX plan for vertical integration?

Mr. ESTEVEZ. Vertical integration is a required, critical capability for any potential EELV new entrant because all current NSS satellites were designed with the expectation that they would be integrated vertically to their launch vehicle. SpaceX agreed that, as a condition of contract award of a NSS launch service, SpaceX must provide data to include a Critical Design Review level design, detailed development and activation schedules, and construction plans for their vertical integration facility. Additionally, SpaceX must demonstrate a vertical integration capability either through a pathfinder activity or vertically integrating a commercial payload prior to the launch of any NSS payload. It is DOD's expectation that SpaceX will meet these requirements if they are awarded a NSS launch service contract.

General SHELTON. SpaceX is working in conjunction with the Air Force on implementing their vertical integration plan.

NASA USE OF THE ATLAS V

40. Senator SESSIONS. Mr. Lightfoot, while you were the Director at the Marshall Space Flight Center, you started the National Institute for Rocket Propulsion Systems (NIRPS). Does NIRPS have the people with the skills and experience to assist the Air Force in this effort to develop a domestic replacement for the RD–180 Russian engine?

Mr. LIGHTFOOT. National Institute for Rocket Propulsion Systems (NIRPS) personnel have the skills and experience to assist the U.S. Air Force in an effort to develop a domestic replacement for the RD–180 engine. NIRPS is a small group of specialists assembled to help preserve and align Government and private rocket propulsion capabilities to meet present and future U.S. civil and defense needs, and to provide authoritative insight and recommendations to National decision authorities. Should the United States choose to pursue the development of a domestic replacement for the RD–180 engine, NASA is prepared to assist as directed. It should be noted, however, that—per administration policy—NASA is not planning to build a replacement for the RD–180. The Agency is pleased that ULA and Blue Origin have decided to partner and to pursue the development of a domestic "boost phase" rocket engine. This engine will join the ranks of other commercially developed US rocket engines used for "boost phase," such as the Merlin 1D developed by SpaceX, and the RS–68, funded by Boeing, once its development and testing is complete.

41. Senator SESSIONS. Mr. Lightfoot, if we are to meet the aggressive timelines necessary to replace the RD–180 by the end of the decade, we will need the support of our Nation's best and brightest. Do I have a commitment from NASA, if provided adequate resources from DOD, to be helpful to the Air Force and DOD in the development of a replacement for the RD–180 Russian engine?

Mr. LIGHTFOOT. Should the United States choose to pursue the development of a domestic replacement for the RD–180 engine, NASA is prepared to assist as directed. As noted above, per administration policy, NASA is not currently planning to build a replacement for the RD–180.

42. Senator SESSIONS. Mr. Lightfoot, it is my understanding that NASA depends upon the Atlas V with its RD–180 engine for a number of its science missions and that it is the identified launch vehicle for two of the three commercial crew supply proposals. How would not having access to the RD–180 impact NASA's plans for ensuring competition in the commercial crew program?

Mr. LIGHTFOOT. In September, NASA awarded contracts to Boeing and SpaceX for commercial crew transportation system certification and transportation services to the ISS. The companies were required to provide a transportation solution that met our NASA safety and performance requirements, including the provision of risk mitigation plans for their solutions. Boeing proposed using the Atlas V launch vehicle with the RD–180 engine as part of its transportation solution. The companies are required to provide a service and they are responsible for planning for and resolving disruptions in their supply chain, which includes their launch vehicle and engine solution. NASA evaluated each company's proposal and selected them based on their ability to meet the CCtCap requirements. We cannot publicly provide additional details of the selection decision or the companies' mitigation plans at this time as the CCtiCap awards are currently part of a protest with the GAO. We expect a GAO decision in early January.

———

QUESTIONS SUBMITTED BY SENATOR DAVID VITTER

NASA SPACE LAUNCH SYSTEM

61. Senator VITTER. Mr. Lightfoot, given the problems with obtaining Russian engines for the military's satellite launches, it is time to develop our own rocket. Years of development and testing are leading up the NASA SLS, which will be the largest rocket ever made, is well on its way to be ready for its first launch in 2017. Within that program there are a great set of talented and experienced staff on hand. There is expertise in manufacturing at the Michoud Assembly Facility, propulsion at the Marshall Space Center, and testing at the Stennis Space Center, and that means we have the personnel who can design, build, test, and complete a new rocket engine. Also, I believe that having the Air Force and NASA cooperate on this endeavor would bring the best minds together and save money by pooling talent and resources. Do you agree that the Air Force and NASA could effectively cooperate in developing a new rocket engine for our Nation's needs?

Mr. LIGHTFOOT. Should the United States choose to pursue the development of a domestic replacement for the RD–180 engine, NASA is prepared to assist as directed. It should be noted, however, that—per administration policy—NASA is not planning to build a replacement for the RD–180. The Agency is pleased that ULA and Blue Origin have decided to partner and to pursue the development of a domestic boost phase rocket engine. This engine will join the ranks of other commercially developed U.S. rocket engines used for boost phase, such as the Merlin 1D developed by SpaceX, and the RS–68, funded by Boeing, once its development and testing is complete.

62. Senator VITTER. Mr. Lightfoot, additionally, SLS is performing well across the board, and I strongly feel that SLS resources should not be diverted, which would slow important progress and delay the program's goals and the launch schedule. With separate budget priorities and Congress reimbursing NASA for involvement and cooperation with the Air Force to address this obvious need, would NASA object to bringing all skills and capability to solve this critical NSS problem?

Mr. LIGHTFOOT. Should the United States choose to pursue the development of a domestic replacement for the RD–180 engine, NASA is prepared to assist as directed. It should be noted, however, that—per administration policy—NASA is not planning to build a replacement for the RD–180. The Agency is pleased that ULA and Blue Origin have decided to partner and to pursue the development of a domestic boost phase rocket engine. This engine will join the ranks of other commercially developed U.S. rocket engines used for boost phase, such as the Merlin 1D developed by SpaceX, and the RS–68, funded by Boeing, once its development and testing is complete.

DAMAGE TO CARGO RETURNING FROM THE INTERNATIONAL SPACE STATION

63. Senator VITTER. Mr. Lightfoot, reports indicate SpaceX has encountered sea water intrusions into their reusable Dragon capsule on all three of their splashdown landings when returning cargo from the ISS, but NASA has yet to provide a conclusive answer regarding damage and has so far given no additional information about these reports. As we consider the issues of access to space, Congress should have the information necessary to provide proper oversight of the work done by government contractors. What equipment was damaged and what is the cost?

Mr. LIGHTFOOT. Regarding water intrusions experienced during the three SpaceX contracted Commercial Resupply Services (CRS) missions, SpaceX experienced water intrusions in the avionics bay of the Dragon capsule on two instances during splashdown. On the first instance, power was lost to the General Laboratory Active Cryogenic ISS Experiment Refrigerator (GLACIER) that contained laboratory samples. Even though power was lost, the samples were not damaged as their temperature did not fall below temperature limits. On the second occasion, water again was experienced in the avionics bay, but no anomalies occurred and the GLACIER maintained power.

On the third incident, water intrusion was experience in the pressurized cargo compartment. The root cause has been determined to be unexpected high pressures seen on the hatch caused by rough seas, landing orientation and wind conditions. A small percentage of NASA cargo did sustain contamination from the saltwater exposure. ISSP is still evaluating the overall cost impacts to the contamination and has not completed the final payment to SpaceX for the mission while it finalizes the estimate.

64. Senator VITTER. Mr. Lightfoot, why was Congress not notified of this damage?

Mr. LIGHTFOOT. NASA is still evaluating the extent of the seawater contamination.

65. Senator VITTER. Mr. Lightfoot, has an Aeronautical Safety Advisory Review Panel inquiry taken place?

Mr. LIGHTFOOT. The ASAP has not been briefed on the results yet as NASA is evaluating the contaminated cargo and SpaceX's overall mission performance. The anomaly was discussed with the ASAP as part of an overall ISS status.

66. Senator VITTER. Mr. Lightfoot, it is to be noted that the NASA Inspector General (IG) has glossed over much of this. Do we know if the IG has done an investigation since mention was made of the first leak in an IG report?

Mr. LIGHTFOOT. The anomalies that our CRS providers SpaceX and Orbital are experiencing are within the experience based on NASA directed programs and the broader industry. The NASA IG has not done an investigation. NASA maintains that these types of anomalies are within family for human spaceflight mission that utilize water landing.

67. Senator VITTER. Mr. Lighfoot, are NASA and the taxpayers being refunded for damaged cargo?

Mr. LIGHTFOOT. Please see response to Question #63, above. No biological samples were damaged or lost during any of the SpaceX missions.

CARGO RESUPPLY MISSIONS SUFFERED SIGNIFICANT FAILURES

68. Senator VITTER. General Shelton, according to reports, SpaceX's three cargo resupply missions for NASA have suffered significant failures, including the loss of an engine on ascent, which resulted in the loss of a satellite; computer malfunctions; thruster failures; the Dragon capsule going into a spin; and the Dragon capsule leaking sea water and damaging cargo, yet NASA has not disclosed any details of these reports. Space travel involved dangerous and harsh environments, yet lesser occurrences have grounded military jets and commercial airlines to find the root cause of the issue to prevent loss of life and property. Would any of the incidents I listed, such as loss of an engine, loss of guidance, or loss of control, require the launch vehicle in question to be grounded by DOD?

General SHELTON. Yes. As you mentioned, space travel is very challenging, involves harsh environments and the fact that we only get one chance to get it right. All launch vehicle incidents or non-conformances are taken very seriously and every effort is made to assess the risk, to include determining root cause, prior to launch.

The Air Force tracks all incidents and non-conformances throughout the design, production, and launch operations. As these items are discovered, we work closely with the launch vehicle contractor to determine root cause, impacts, and closure plan in order to ensure a successful mission. After a launch, we accomplish an extensive post-flight review of mission data looking for any incidents or out-of-family data to ensure there are no concerns for the next mission. If an incident such as the ones you mentioned were to occur, we would implement the anomaly resolution process to guide the forward plan and delay future launches, if necessary, until it is resolved.

For DOD launches, the integrated U.S. Government/Industry team would evaluate the incidents listed to determine impacts and root cause. The evaluation would result in corrective actions required for the launch vehicle supplier to maintain Space Flight Worthiness Certification. Space Flight Worthiness measures the degree to which a spacecraft, launch vehicle, or critical ground system, as constituted, has the capability to perform its mission with the confidence that significant risks are known and deemed acceptable.

69. Senator VITTER. General Shelton, what is the process DOD uses to return a launch vehicle to active status?

General SHELTON. There are two Return To Flight (RTF) certification processes: safety assurance and mission assurance. The Launch Base Space Wing Commander is the designated authority for certifying safety RTF. The Space and Missile Systems Center Commander is the designated authority for certifying mission assurance RTF for Air Force missions and Air Force-managed payload and launch vehicles in support of non-Air Force customers. Following any launch mishap, if the mishap is launch system-related, applicable safety RTF criteria must be addressed before the system in question is allowed to launch from an AFSPC space launch range. Additionally, if the mishap is range safety-related or if range safety procedures failed to adequately protect the public or government personnel during a launch, the safety RTF criteria must be addressed before any launch can occur from an AFSPC space launch range. Mission assurance RTF criteria must be addressed prior to the next Air Force-supported mission utilizing the launch vehicle, payload, subsystem, component, aerospace ground equipment, or procedure having contributed to a launch mishap.

Safety RTF criteria are established to ensure that range safety system operation is not affected by the mishap, risk analyses are still valid, and that all other considerations which could affect launch risk are addressed and mitigated. At a minimum, it includes verification of the Flight Termination System, verification the range safety systems did not contribute to or cause the mishap, or that failures in these systems have been corrected to eliminate such contributions, ensures hazard/risk assessments were adequate, evaluation of range operations, and ensure appropriate measures have been taken to control the most likely failure cause.

Mission Assurance RTF criteria focus on ensuring successful mission execution and establishing an acceptable technical risk baseline for Space Flight Worthiness Certification. At a minimum, it includes ensuring all failure-related issues involving pre-launch processing are resolved, ensuring all failure-related issues involving launch vehicle and/or payload performance go/no-go criteria are resolved, ensuring all failure-related issues involving launch vehicle and/or payload hardware production, integration, and test, vehicle inspection/checkout, or contractor processes/procedures are resolved, and ensuring all failure-related issues involving launch vehicle and/or payload design flaws are resolved.

70. Senator VITTER. General Shelton, what are the checks and balances to ensure the technical issue has been properly addressed and approximately how long does this process take? Please provide me an example of a recent return to flight process to use as a benchmark.

General SHELTON. The Air Force EELV Mission Assurance process, which has many checks and balances, establishes a technical risk baseline for Space Flight Worthiness certification. All technical issues are addressed with this process. It is comprised of three areas: (1) nonrecurring qualification activities that confirm the system design meets requirements and can demonstrate the necessary margins, the manufacturing processes are appropriate and repeatable, and test hardware works after qualification; (2) recurring verification of flight hardware conformance to qualifications; and (3) anomaly resolution and corresponding risk assessments for nonconformances and technical issues. The EELV Mission Assurance process includes the Air Force, Aerospace Corporation, Space and Missile Center's Independent Readiness Review Team, and the Launch Vehicle Contractor.

The nonrecurring efforts are performed mainly during the launch vehicle design and qualification which occurs over several years. Portions of the nonrecurring effort can be re-accomplished to address any design changes and can be accomplished within weeks to months.

The recurring effort is conducted for each individual mission and includes many different tasks from validating launch environments to evaluation of mission unique requirements. These efforts occur over the 2 year launch integration contract period.

The anomaly resolution effort evaluates the unpredicted technical issues that arise during design, production, and launch operations. Air Force, Aerospace Corporation, and launch vehicle contractor responsible engineers monitor the design, production, and launch operations and identify technical issues and nonconformances that need to enter the review process. The issues are reviewed by four independent engineering boards: (1) Launch Vehicle Contractor; (2) Air Force Chief Engineer; (3) Aerospace Corporation; and (4) Space and Missile Center's Independent Readiness Review Team. This process can take anywhere from hours to years depending on the resolution required to maintain or achieve Space Flight Worthiness Certification.

Specifically, to address your request for an example of a return-to-flight process, during the October 2012 launch of GPS IIF–3, a fuel leak occurred within the upper stage engine. Even though the mission was a success, the in-flight anomaly delayed launches of the Atlas V and Delta IV fleet in order to evaluate the anomaly. As the investigation progressed, information gathered allowed the independent engineering boards to determine a mission-by-mission acceptable risk level for Atlas V return-to-flight in December 2012 and was based on engineering and operational differences between the Atlas V and Delta IV upper stage engines. Delta IV mission-by-mission return-to-flight was achieved in May 2013. Atlas V and Delta IV fleet clearance was achieved in July 2014, almost 2 years from the initial anomaly.

71. Senator VITTER. General Shelton, are these anomalies taken into consideration in the certification process?

General SHELTON. Yes, the Air Force began early insight efforts with SpaceX and observation of the Falcon 9 v1.0 missions, to include the Commercial Resupply Services missions, which have informed the certification process, and the Air Force has observed and will continue to observe every flight of the Falcon 9 v1.1 launch system while undergoing certification. We continue to work with SpaceX, within their anomaly resolution process, to reach concurrence on root cause of any anomaly and the implemented resolution for the fleet of vehicles and for the next flight.

72. Senator VITTER. General Shelton, can you assure me that no efforts are being made inside or outside DOD to skirt this process?

General SHELTON. Yes, the Air Force is following the NECG and working through the signed CRADA with SpaceX. No efforts are being made inside or outside DOD to bypass this process.

NATIONAL SECURITY SPACE LAUNCH

73. Senator LEE. Mr. Estevez, this committee has been clear, that for national security purposes, it desires the development of a domestic replacement of the RD–180 so that we do not have to rely on Russia for certain launch capabilities. I believe that DOD should not be focused solely on liquid replacements for the RD–180 and future rocket systems, but should have an open competition that looks at all domestically produced capabilities, including solid rocket motors, to determine the system that provides the best cost-benefit for the government. Do you believe that DOD would benefit from considering other types of propulsion systems and allowing a fair and open competition that includes solid and liquid solutions when looking to domestically replace the RD–180 engine and for future launch systems?

Mr. ESTEVEZ. I do believe DOD would benefit from considering other types of propulsion systems. A Request for Information (RFI), released by the Air Force on August 21, 2014, seeks industry inputs on a broad range of launch capabilities, to include booster propulsion systems and/or launch systems; it does not constrain itself to liquid propulsion systems. The industry input we have received in response to this RFI will be critical in shaping DOD's planning on this critical issue.

74. Senator LEE. General Shelton, this committee included report language in the National Defense Authorization Act for Fiscal Year 2015 regarding domestically produced rocket engines, stating that propulsion systems in addition to liquid rocket engines could provide future capabilities that support DOD requirements for medium or heavy launch vehicles, and recommends that DOD continually review the potential of using such propulsion systems. DOD is also required by the provision to report to the committee on the feasibility of using other propulsion systems in addition to liquid engines. Would you please give me an update on the status of this report and your thoughts on the usability of other propulsion systems like solid rocket motors for NSS launch?

General SHELTON. Solid rocket motors (SRM) are one course of action that the DOD is considering in mitigating reliance on the RD–180. The Air Force released a Request for Information (RFI) on August 20, 2014, seeking additional data on potential alternative propulsion systems. Industry may include SRMs as a potential course of action that may be provided in response to the RFI. RFI responses are due back to the Air Force on September 19, 2014. The report is still in work, and will be delivered as part of the full-scale engine development effort plan from the Secretary of the Air Force in coordination with the NASA Administrator.

75. Senator LEE. Mr. Estevez and General Shelton, do you believe that it is in the national security interest of the United States for DOD to continue to ensure that we maintain a domestic source of the critical chemical ammonium perchlorate used in space launches and tactical and ballistic missiles?

Mr. ESTEVEZ. Yes, I do believe that ammonium perchlorate is important. Within DOD, both the Defense Logistics Agency (DLA) Strategic Materials and USD(AT&L)/Manufacturing and Industrial Base Policy organizations are closely monitoring the needs of the defense industrial base regarding ammonium perchlorate and its associated supply. Specifically, ammonium perchlorate is among over 160 materials which compose a Watch List of materials of concern for the defense industrial base which was created by the Director of DLA Strategic Materials with input from industry and key government stakeholders, such as the DOD Critical Energetic Materials Working Group and the Joint Army-Navy-NASA-Air Force (JAANAF) Programmatic and Industrial Base Committee. These organizations collaborate to analyze, prioritize, and make informed decisions regarding all strategically important materials that may bear on national security, and will do so in the case of ammonium perchlorate.

This year, DOD initiated a study to address concerns with ammonium perchlorate. The objective of the study is to develop mitigation alternatives that reduce the cost and schedule risks for DOD. Alternatives should include identifying approaches to reduce capacity in the existing facility and analyzing cost and schedule for development of a new right-sized facility. Reducing the re-qualification cost burden for DOD weapons systems that experience an ingredient change also is being addressed. We expect to see results from this effort in the second quarter of fiscal year 2015. DOD has the necessary authorities to deal with this issue.

General SHELTON. Yes, solid rocket propulsion is a key enabler across several aspects of national security.

SPACE LAUNCH COMPETITION AND CERTIFICATION

43. Senator MCCAIN. Mr. Estevez, it was recently announced that the Air Force approved three flights that the new entrant has performed to show the Air Force of its capability for military payload launches. Please describe in detail what steps remain for certification of new entrants, the expected dates for these steps to occur, and whether these steps are the primary responsibility of the government or of the new entrant.

Mr. ESTEVEZ. As part of the NECG and CRADA, the new entrant chose a certification approach that requires both launches as well as government evaluation of characteristics of their launch system. These characteristics include, for example: design reliability, manufacturing operations, test and verification processes, quality processes, and risk management processes. The new entrant must successfully pass three gate reviews prior to certification. Gate 1 occurs at the end of the System Assessment Phase; Gate 2 at the end of the System Evaluation Phase; and Gate 3 at the end of the Certification Phase. After the Gate 3 review, the Air Force makes a certification determination. For the SpaceX Falcon9v1.1, the Assessment Phase Gate 1 review was conducted on June 27, 2014, with the Air Force providing approval (with liens) for entry into the next phase on August 7, 2014. The Falcon9v1.1 Evaluation and Certification Phase activities, currently underway, are running concurrently and the Gate 2 and Gate 3 reviews were combined into a single review; that review was held on December 8, 2014. At this time, we expect the Air Force will complete its certification determination within the next 120 days.

RUSSIAN ENGINES

44. Senator MCCAIN. Mr. Estevez, regarding EELV's Russian engine, the Government Accountability Office (GAO) noted a serious lack of transparency of EELV components in a recent March 2014 report that said: "DOD may have lacked sufficient knowledge to negotiate fair and reasonable launch prices." With this in mind, how has DOD concluded that cost and pricing of these engines is now fair and reasonable?

Mr. ESTEVEZ. The RD–180 engines were determined by the contracting officer to be commercial items in accordance with Federal Acquisition Regulation (FAR) 15.403–1(c)(3). Acquisitions of any supply or service deemed commercial are exempted from the requirement for certified cost or pricing data in accordance with 10 USC 2306a and FAR 15.403–1(b)(3). Commercial items are evaluated using price analysis in accordance with FAR 15.404–1(a)(2). Price analysis is the process of examining and evaluating a proposed price without evaluating its separate cost elements and proposed profit.

As part of the price analysis of the RD–180 engines supplied to ULA under its subcontract with RD AMROSS, the Air Force first compared proposed prices for RD–180 rocket engines to historical prices paid. The Air Force then correlated and compared the RD–180 engine price to the Pratt & Whitney Rocketdyne (now Aerojet Rocketdyne) built RS–68 engine for the Delta IV launch vehicle. The final method used was to compare the prices to the results of a Should Cost Study for a Pratt & Whitney co-produced RD–180. This method used a bottoms-up estimate of the entire effort required to establish co-production of the RD–180 engine in the United States in lieu of in Russia. The price analysis justified the fairness and reasonableness of the RD–180 engine prices being charged to ULA by RD AMROSS, and ultimately to the Air Force. Nonetheless, we continue to assess the price reasonableness of the RD–180 engine.

GLOBAL POSITIONING SYSTEM SATELLITES

45. Senator MCCAIN. General Shelton, the new GPS version III satellites the Air Force has decided to delay gives increased GPS capability to our warfighters compared to what they have today. Are GPS version III satellites needed by our troops to fulfill a validated operational requirement for our combatant commanders to have protected and improved positioning technology, and if this is the case, what is the impact to the warfighters and the combatant commanders of not having this capability?

General SHELTON. Yes. GPS III is very important to both the sustainment of a healthy GPS constellation and the deployment of M-code capability to improve GPS military capability in jamming environments. Not having M-code makes it easier for an adversary to deny our use of GPS. The current constellation plan provides the capability for M-code on schedule to meet the fiscal year 2017 congressional requirement (National Defense Authorization Act for Fiscal Year 2011).

———

COST OF TRANSPORTATION TO AND FROM THE INTERNATIONAL SPACE STATION

46. Senator AYOTTE. Mr. Lightfoot, how much do we pay to the Russians to get our astronauts to and from the ISS?

Mr. LIGHTFOOT. In April 2014, NASA contracted with the Russian Federal Space Agency (Roscosmos) on a sole-source basis for six Soyuz seats and associated services for calendar year 2017 with rescue and return services extending through spring 2018 via contract modification. Services include all necessary training and preparation for launch, flight operations, return and rescue of U.S. or U.S.-designated astronauts and associated services. The seat price is approximately $76.0 million and is ~8 percent higher than the last contract modification.

RD–180 REPLACEMENT

47. Senator AYOTTE. Mr. Estevez, in your written statement, you state that, "DOD believes the Nation needs to eliminate our utilization of Russian propulsion systems in the most efficient and affordable manner." Why do you believe that this is necessary?

Mr. ESTEVEZ. The current situation between Russia and Ukraine obviously causes DOD concern. The Government of Russia could choose to unilaterally interrupt the supply of RD–180 engines which would seriously impact our space launch capability. DOD takes any risk to our assured access to space seriously and is looking at options to insulate the Nation from this possibility.

48. Senator AYOTTE. General Shelton, in your prepared statement, you discuss the Air Force's recently completed RD–180 Availability Risk Mitigation Study. You state that the study found that an RD–180 production loss or interruption would have "significant impact on our ability to reliably launch the current manifest of NSS payloads on a schedule of our choosing." Would you please provide more details on the impact on U.S. space capabilities and NSS if there is an interruption in the RD–180 supply?

General SHELTON. The RD–180 Availability Risk Mitigation Study showed the cost impact ranges from $2.5 billion to $5 billion, depending on when the United States would be cut off from using the RD–180. The manifest impacts range from needing to remanifest nine missions with an average launch delay of 2 years, to the more severe case of needing to remanifest 31 missions with an average launch delay of 3.5 years. Consideration would have to be taken regarding the NSS priority of each payload in order to mitigate the impact to NSS. There would also be potential impacts to NASA and commercial missions.

49. Senator AYOTTE. General Shelton, what would be the benefits of a domestically produced new engine program?

General SHELTON. A new domestically-produced engine would eliminate our reliance on a foreign-made booster engine, would enable our technological advancement, and would stimulate the industrial base, resulting in more competitive U.S. launch capabilities in the future.

DUPLICATION BETWEEN DOD AND NASA

50. Senator AYOTTE. Ms. Chaplain, since 2012, you have cited space launch contract costs as an area of government duplication. GAO has argued that increased collaboration between DOD and NASA could reduce launch contracting duplication. Would you please explain areas of duplication between DOD and NASA that could be eliminated in order to save money?

Ms. CHAPLAIN. In 2012. GAO reported that the government is not acting as a single buyer and therefore its investment in launch acquisitions may not be optimized. DOD and NASA currently negotiate and contract for launch services separately, though they are contracting with the same company as one another. This arrangement may not leverage the government's overall negotiating power to get the best prices for launch services from launch service providers. For example, when negotiating the new block buy contract with ULA, the Air Force did not include NASA's launch needs for the contract's duration into the negotiations. Had NASA's needs been included in the negotiations, the additional launch quantities included in the contract might have helped bring prices down even farther. Similarly, since NASA launches were not included in the block buy, NASA will negotiate contracts with ULA separately, under NASA's own contracting structure. NASA currently has contracts with both SpaceX and Orbital Sciences Corporation for space station resupply missions. If the Air Force begins awarding EELV launch services contracts to either or both of these companies, they will be negotiating separately from NASA for these contracts. In addition, there may be other instances of duplication between DOD and NASA in the launch area, such as mission assurance, test assets, and launch workforces, but we have not looked at them specifically.

RD–180 ENGINE SUPPLY DISRUPTION

51. Senator AYOTTE. Mr. Estevez, General Shelton, and Mr. Lightfoot, if a disruption in the supply of the RD–180 engines occurs and we have to prioritize space launches based on national security, how will this affect civilian and commercial launches?

Mr. ESTEVEZ. In the event a supply disruption occurs, all affected parties will first utilize the Current Launch Schedule Review Board (CLSRB) process to work together to find a mutually acceptable solution. If all parties are unable to reach agreement in the Air Force-led CLSRB, the issue will be raised to the interagency process for adjudication at the interdepartmental level.

Because the timing of a disruption has significant influence on the actual impacts, it is difficult to quantify the potential effects to individual users. The CLSRB and the interagency review process will seek to balance national security needs with the civil and commercial users in a manner that results in the best solution for the Nation as a whole.

General SHELTON. To date, we have not seen any disruptions in supply of the RD–180. Effects from any potential disruptions would depend heavily on the specific timing and conditions of any supply disruption. Prioritization of space launch missions would occur through the standing CLSRB, which includes membership from the Services, DOD agencies, NASA, and launch service providers.

Mr. LIGHTFOOT. If such a disruption were to occur, there would be an impact on all missions that have an on-contract Atlas V launch service, not just civil and commercial missions. However, the magnitude of the impact would be greatly dependent on the timing and the circumstances of the disruption. NASA would expect to engage in a prioritization discussion with our DOD colleagues for the allocation of in-country RD–180 engines to on-contract Atlas V launch service missions. Any NASA Atlas V on-contract missions not allocated an RD–180 engine would then need to move to Delta IV or Falcon 9. The cost for moving an on-contract mission would be dependent on the timing and circumstances for that mission. For NASA satellite missions that have yet to award the contract for a launch service requiring an "Atlas V-class" lift performance, the ULA Delta IV and SpaceX Falcon 9 v1.1 would be competitive options.

BLOCK BUY

52. Senator AYOTTE. General Shelton, when the Air Force initiated the 36 core block buy, how much weight was given to the potential for new certified launch providers?

General SHELTON. A significant amount of weight was given to the potential for certification of a new entrant. The quantity for the 36-core block buy was determined through a three-pronged analysis approach conducted in the summer/fall 2012.

The first prong was the space vehicle assessment. This assessment was designed to determine how many satellites would require launching between fiscal year 2015 to fiscal year 2019. Launch vehicles are nominally ordered 2 years prior to the projected launch date (3 years for a heavy launch vehicle). This assessment concluded that 50 launch vehicle booster cores were required to be purchased between fiscal year 2013 to fiscal year 2017 to meet the operational requirements.

The second prong was the New Entrant Readiness Assessment. This assessment was designed to determine when one or more of the emerging new launch providers would be certified to launch EELV-class missions and which type of NSS satellites their launch systems could lift. The Air Force commissioned an independent team to conduct this assessment. Primarily based on the new entrant's own schedule, they concluded that the earliest a new entrant would be available for award of a launch vehicle (core) contract would be fiscal year 2015, with the first launch of

EELV-class missions no earlier than fiscal year 2017. Additionally, this assessment stated that the SpaceX produced Falcon 9v1.1 launch vehicle was the most mature new entrant launch system that would meet certification within the fiscal year 2013 to fiscal year 2017 timeframe. However, the Falcon 9v1.1 is only capable of lifting the lower portion of the EELV lift requirement, referred to as medium class missions. The heavier portion of the EELV lift requirement, intermediate and heavy class missions, can currently only be performed by ULA.

The third prong was the Air Force assessment of the ULA proposed quantity and length of commitment options. Per the RFP the Air Force submitted to ULA in March 2012, the Air Force requested ULA provide prices for launch vehicle booster core commitments ranging from 6 to 10 cores per year over 3-, 4-, and 5-year periods. ULA proposed if the Air Force committed to procuring at least 40 cores over 5 years, ULA would procure an additional 10 cores and pass the quantities of scale savings to the Air Force. ULA later agreed to procure 14 additional cores for a total of 50 with an Air Force commitment of 36 cores over 5 years and still pass those quantity discount savings to the Air Force.

The assimilation of these three assessments led to the conclusion that a 36-core commitment over 5 years to ULA provided a significant price break over previous procurement practices while still providing competitive missions opportunities to potential certified new entrants. At that time, the first 16 of those 36 cores were expected to be awarded before any new entrant would be certified. The other 20 were identified as having mission requirements that could only be met by ULA.

53. Senator AYOTTE. General Shelton, what cost estimates did you conduct to come to the conclusion that a 36 core block buy would be most financially advantageous?

General SHELTON. Through the analysis of historical program actuals, detailed technical evaluations, implementation of Better Buying Power principles, and tough negotiations, the government was able to realize significant cost reductions to the annual cost of launch. The quantity for the 36-core block buy was determined through a 3-pronged analysis approach conducted in the summer/fall 2012.

The first prong was the space vehicle assessment. This assessment was designed to determine how many satellites would require launching between fiscal year 2015 to fiscal year 2019. Launch vehicles are nominally ordered 2 years prior to the projected launch date (3 years for a heavy launch vehicle). This assessment concluded that 50 launch vehicle booster cores were required to be purchased between fiscal year 2013 to fiscal year 2017 to meet the operational requirements.

The second prong was the New Entrant Readiness Assessment. This assessment was designed to determine when one or more of the emerging new launch providers would be certified to launch EELV-class missions and which type of NSS satellites their launch systems could lift. The Air Force commissioned an independent team to conduct this assessment. Their assessment concluded that the earliest a new entrant would procure a launch vehicle would be fiscal year 2015 with the first launch of EELV-class missions no earlier than fiscal year 2017. Additionally, this assessment stated that the SpaceX produced Falcon 9v1.1 launch vehicle was the most mature new entrant launch system that would meet certification with in the fiscal year 2013 to fiscal year 2017 timeframe. The Falcon 9v1.1 is only capable of lifting the lower portion of the EELV lift requirement, referred to as medium class missions. The heavier portion of the EELV lift requirement, intermediate and heavy class missions, could only be performed by ULA, as well as missions to be procured in fiscal year 2013 to fiscal year 2014, totaling 36 cores. At that time, the first 16 of those cores were expected to be awarded before any new entrants would be certified. The other 20 were identified as having mission requirements that could only be met by ULA. Based on this analysis, up to 14 cores were identified for potential competition, within the fiscal year 2015 to fiscal year 2017 timeframe.

The third prong was the Air Force assessment, which proposed quantity and length of commitment options. The Air Force received a proposal from ULA in 2013 with pricing points for commitment periods of 3 to 5 years and quantities of 6 to 10 cores per year. ULA offered a price discount if a 5-year commitment of 8 cores per year was made. Prior to negotiations, the Air Force conducted extensive cost analysis, including a complete technical deep dive of all major subcontractors and the prime, site visits, DCMA involvement, and cost and price analysis. Through negotiations, the Air Force obtained better pricing than ULA's discounted offer for the 36 cores referenced above.

The assimilation of these assessments led to the conclusion that a 36-core commitment over 5 years to ULA provided a substantial price break over previous procurement practices, while still providing competitive missions opportunities to potential certified new entrants.

54. Senator AYOTTE. General Shelton, you note that block buy represents a $4.4 billion reduction from baseline in the fiscal year 2012 budget. Reductions from the baseline are only useful if the baseline is accurate. Assuming at least one new launch provider is certified within the timespan of the block buy mission period, what further reductions might we have made—or will make—from that 2012 baseline?

General SHELTON. The $4.4 billion reduction from the baseline in the fiscal year 2012 budget represents a culmination of cost savings achieved through Better-Buying-Power initiatives implemented starting in 2011, such as changing from Cost Plus Award Fee to Cost Plus Incentive Fee contract structure for EELV launch capability, economies of scale pricing from the Phase 1 block buy contract, and stability of the industrial base through the long-term commitment of the block buy. Although the Air Force cannot accurately estimate what savings could be obtained through competition of launch services as each potential bidder will make numerous business decisions in the process of developing bids, further reductions are possible if at least one new launch provider is certified to compete for missions above the block buy baseline. The Air Force will continue its strong, focused efforts to certify new launch providers and promote a competitive environment for launch services.

The strategy for the block buy was to award cores based on analysis that we expected to buy from ULA, given our assessment of new entrant certification efforts. Of the 36 cores awarded, 16 were to be awarded when only ULA was certified. The remaining 20 were for missions only ULA would execute. While the assumption was that a new entrant could be certified and therefore available for fiscal year 2015 awards, as early as 2014, none has yet completed all steps toward certification.

SPACEX ROCKETS

55. Senator AYOTTE. Mr. Estevez, we have been reading reports about the Air Force's rejection of SpaceX's unsolicited bid for GPS III satellites. Disregarding the eligibility requirements the Air Force may have used to reject the bid, is it technically possible to launch the satellites at issue aboard SpaceX rockets? If the answer is no, why not? If the answer is yes, why, and to what degree do current rules and regulations drive up the costs of launches?

Mr. ESTEVEZ. Current analysis indicates that SpaceX Falcon 9v1.1 can lift the GPS III satellite. When the proposal was received, SpaceX was not a certified EELV provider and therefore was not eligible for a launch service contract award. While there is a relatively small cost to both the contractor and the government associated with the certification process, it is critical that DOD ensure all launch service providers meet minimum design reliability requirements. DOD will continue to require that launch services contracts only be issued to certified providers. Insight into the vehicle design developed during the certification process allows DOD to minimize its cost in the long run by maximizing the probability of successfully launching our critical NSS payloads.

DRIVING DOWN COSTS

56. Senator AYOTTE. Mr. Dumbacher, in your testimony you state, "It is clear that cost growth associated with access to space and propulsion is a major threat to the competitive U.S. launch posture. Therefore, it is essential that the U.S. rocket propulsion industry directly and aggressively address launch system costs, working to drive down the cost to develop and operate launch vehicles and propulsion systems." Is competition an effective mechanism for driving down costs in the space launch ecosystem?

Mr. DUMBACHER. Competition is essential to reduce development and operations costs. It is an effective tool and should be used appropriately.

57. Senator AYOTTE. Mr. Dumbacher, does the government's NSS launch certification process drive up costs by reducing competition or does the compliance cost avoid failed launches that would be more costly?

Mr. DUMBACHER. I am not an expert on the NSS launch certification process. This country has learned through tough experience (base realignment and closure in the late 1990s) that sufficient technical and programmatic insight is needed to assure mission success. Loss of mission and loss of vehicle during launch are costly to the success of the industry. However, there is a needed risk based balance among insight, oversight, certification, and use of best commercial practices to assure mission success at an appropriate cost.

COST ASSUMPTIONS

58. Senator AYOTTE. Ms. Chaplain, does the $9.5 billion you mention DOD expects to spend in the next 5 years on the EELV include new launch providers?

Ms. CHAPLAIN. The $9.5 billion figure represents the amount that the Air Force requested in the fiscal year 2014 President's budget. The funding was requested to award contracts for the Air Force's national security space launch manifest over fiscal years 2014 to 2018, among other things. This figure includes launches that the Air Force planned to be launched by the ULA, as well as other launches that they planned to put up for competition between ULA and new entrants. This figure did not include launches funded by other military services or government organizations, such as the Navy or the National Reconnaissance Office. It should be noted that, due to the contract price reductions that the Air Force was able to negotiate with ULA, the fiscal year 2015 President's budget for the same time period was about $7.4 billion.

59. Senator AYOTTE. Ms. Chaplain, either way, what cost assumptions has DOD made regarding new entrants in the provider market?

Ms. CHAPLAIN. We are unaware of any specific cost assumptions that DOD has made regarding new entrants to the launch market.

60. Senator AYOTTE. Ms. Chaplain, General Shelton noted that the block buy represents a $4.4 billion reduction from the baseline in the fiscal year 2012 budget. Reductions from baseline are only useful if the baseline is accurate. What do you think of the potential savings?

Ms. CHAPLAIN. GAO has not independently validated the Air Force's $4.4 billion savings claim. We have reported that DOD took on a significant effort to obtain and analyze contractor and subcontractor data, an important step to strengthening the government's negotiating position and lowering prices. For example, DOD officials and the National Reconnaissance Office cost analysis group collected detailed data on engine prices and subcontractor costs. DOD also scrutinized launch processes to identify and eliminate potentially redundant activities in the new contract. As a result, DOD contracting officials had a stronger bargaining position to lower overall contract costs than in previous negotiations, and through the stable unit pricing they negotiated for all launch vehicles they were able to enjoy lower prices on launch services under the new contract. The threat of potential competition in the EELV launch market also likely provided further bargaining power for the Air Force to reduce launch contract costs.

With regards to the accuracy of the baseline of the 2012 budget, we have not analyzed the information that went into that budget.

○

www.ingramcontent.com/pod-product-compliance
Lightning Source LLC
Chambersburg PA
CBHW081135290526
45795CB00006B/2240